A TIME TO SEEK THE LORD

Fr MICHAEL CAMPBELL OSA

A Time to Seek the Lord

Meditations for Lent

ST PAULS

ST PAULS Publishing
187 Battersea Bridge Road, London SW11 3AS, UK
www.stpauls.ie

ISBN 978 0 85439 740 2

Set by Tukan DTP, Stubbington, Fareham, UK
Printed in Malta by Progress Press Company Limited

ST PAULS is an activity of the priests and brothers
of the Society of St Paul who proclaim the Gospel
through the media of social communication

Contents

To
my confrères in the Augustinian Order

Foreword

Lent has always had an important place in the yearly cycle of the Church's year. Now, I would suggest, we need the Lenten Season more than ever. Life is too full, too busy. There are hundreds of decisions to be made, daily, from the banal to those that have the potential to change our lives and impact on the lives of others. Lent becomes our annual excuse and our reason for reflection. No doubt our busy lives are full of important and worthy duties. We are working hard, providing for our family, looking after our children, living life to the full. And our decisions have to be made. But we can be so busy that we can begin to lose sight of why we do things, what should shape our decisions and our choices. Lent is our invitation to step back and take stock of who we are and what we are about.

In this book, Fr Michael Campbell brings us back to the simple foundation of our faith. He invites us back to the essentials: how Jesus Christ speaks to us through the Scriptures – and how we may respond to his Word. Drawing on the Scripture passages of Mass throughout Lent, Fr Michael's commentary draws us back to the way that God prepared His people for the coming of the Messiah and how that plan is confirmed and completed in all that Jesus teaches and does. Then, acknowledging that each Christian is called on a journey of faith which must include growth and change, the question must be 'What is my response to the Word of God?'

Let us allow this Lent to speak to us of God's loving plan, and challenge us about the way we live our lives.

Bishop John Arnold
Auxiliary Bishop
Westminster diocese

Introduction

The season of Lent has traditionally been understood by the Church as a call directly from God to reflect more deeply on the purpose and direction of our lives. By committing ourselves to the spiritual exercises of Lent we are following the example of Jesus Christ who devoted himself to forty days of prayer, fasting and struggle with temptation in the wilderness. As he prepared for his life's work, Christ felt the need to withdraw in order to be alone with his Father in prolonged prayer, and to reflect profoundly on the future course of his life. During this time he was to experience in the depths of his humanity the full force of the Tempter's seductions, and it gradually became clear to him that the superficial attractions Satan offered would not be in accordance with his Father's will for him. His resistance to temptation remains a permanent encouragement and inspiration to us.

The reflections contained in this book are based on the Scripture readings used by the Church in her daily Lenten liturgy. Prayerful reflection on these inspired texts will enable us to enter more deeply into the spirit of Lent as she prepares to celebrate the paschal mystery of her Lord and Saviour, Jesus Christ. Pondering the words of Holy Scripture as we journey with the Church through these hallowed days towards Easter, God the Father speaks to us as his children. Then we begin to appreciate something of the mystery of Christ's self-abasement and exaltation referred to by St Paul in his Letter to the Philippians, 'Christ Jesus, although he was in the form of God, emptied himself to take the form of a servant … and humbled himself, becoming obedient to death, even death on a cross. But God raised him up…' (see Phil 2:6-9).

'Since we are shortly to celebrate the coming Passion of our crucified Lord, a fitting part of our Lenten devotion should be for us also to make a cross for ourselves by curbing the desires of the flesh, as the Apostle says, *"Those who belong to Christ Jesus have crucified their flesh with its passions and desires."* (Gal 5:24) The Christian ought to hang continually on this cross his whole life long, a life which is lived in the midst of temptations.' (St Augustine, Sermon 205, 1)

Meditations

ASH WEDNESDAY TO SATURDAY

ASH WEDNESDAY

Readings: Joel 2:12-18; 2 Corinthians 5:20-6:2;
Matthew 6:1-6,16-18

*Behold now is the acceptable time. Behold today is the
day of salvation.*

2 Corinthians 6:2

The three great pillars of Lent are set clearly before us
by the Lord in the Gospel of Ash Wednesday: prayer,
fasting and almsgiving. We are to engage in these
spiritual activities quietly and with an absence of outward
show. They are to come from the heart where God
alone can see and judge, and who will reward us at the
appropriate time. The prophet Joel, in summoning Israel
to repentance, calls us to rend our hearts and not our
garments, stressing that genuine religion must touch
what is deepest within us.

These aspects of the Christian life highlighted by the
Lord Jesus capture the essence of the Lenten season. In
devoting ourselves to prayer we are giving God the
first place in our lives, acknowledging our dependence
on him and the need of his help. The discipline of
fasting teaches us that there is more to us than the
satisfaction of our bodily demands. Properly understood,
fasting leads us to acknowledge our spiritual nature and
the values which transcend the mere material. The

duty of almsgiving reminds us that our Lenten exercises are incomplete if we ignore the poor of our world. The twin foundations of our faith must always be love of God, expressed in love of our neighbour.

St Paul, in the extract from his Second Letter to the Corinthians, exhorts us to embrace gladly this time of grace. Lent is intended above all to be a season of God's favour and graciousness to us.

THURSDAY AFTER ASH WEDNESDAY

Readings: Deuteronomy 30:15-20; Luke 9:22-25

Behold, I set before you today life and prosperity, death and disaster.

Deuteronomy 30:15

Both our readings today, appropriately for Lent, enjoin us to choose life. Moses has led the people of Israel through the wilderness for forty years and they now stand on the verge of the land of promise. As they prepare to move into a new future he declares that two paths lie open before them: the first under God will lead to life and blessing, the second, following other gods, is the path to death. Israel's survival and prosperity depended on her loyalty and fidelity to the covenant, expressed in the commandments and the Law of Moses. The temptation to wander and find refuge in the worship of pagan gods would be strong and persistent, but one that for their own sake and that of their children they must resist. The words of Moses over three thousand years ago have lost none of their force and continue to reverberate down to the present day: 'Choose life!'

If the follower of Jesus wishes to choose life it will necessarily involve sharing in his cross. The unique paradox of Christian discipleship consists in dying to ourselves so as to attain true life. In this respect the disciple is not greater than his master (Jn 13:16). Throughout the Gospels Christ speaks clearly of his ultimate fate, when he would be rejected, suffer, be put to death and rise to life again on the third day. Our Christian life begins in baptism when we become one with Christ in his death and Resurrection. That drama of death and Resurrection, we are forcibly reminded in this Lenten Gospel, must be enacted daily in the life of each baptised Christian. It is by dying in Christ to sin and selfishness that we discover the meaning of true living.

FRIDAY AFTER ASH WEDNESDAY

Readings: Isaiah 58:1-9; Matthew 9:14-15

Then you will call and the Lord will answer. You will cry out and he will respond, 'Behold I am here'.

Isaiah 58:9

The subject of both our Scripture readings today is fasting. The prophet Isaiah distinguishes the kind of fast which finds favour with God from fasting which is merely superficial and not reflective of a true religious spirit. True fasting must be accompanied by righteous behaviour and a sense of justice towards others. Our religious practices will bring down God's blessings provided we accept responsibility for the oppressed and deprived in society. Isaiah here may be said to anticipate Christ's insistence that love of God and love of neighbour are indissolubly linked. A genuine love of God will necessarily reach out to others, especially those in need of a helping hand.

In our Gospel passage Jesus is asked why his disciples don't fast, like those of John and the Pharisees. At first sight Christ's reply appears enigmatic. Describing himself in a favoured biblical image as the bridegroom, he states that now is not the time for fasting. In other words, with the presence of the Word made flesh the betrothal of God and his people, long promised by the prophets, has now come to pass. A wedding celebration is an occasion of joy, hardly the time for fasting.

Christ's disciples will fast, however, when he is taken away from them. The pain and distress attached to his coming suffering and death may be compared to a time of fasting for his disciples. And God's people are in some sense fasting as they await the final return of the divine bridegroom for the consummation of the wedding feast

SATURDAY AFTER ASH WEDNESDAY

Readings: Isaiah 58: 9-14; Luke 5:27-32

I did not come to call the righteous, but rather sinners to
repentance.

Luke 5:32

In a passage, lyrical in tone, Isaiah lays before Israel the favourable consequences of sincere religious observance accompanied by an active social conscience. Almighty God is deeply concerned for the welfare and prosperity of his people, and should they remain faithful to their covenantal obligations they will inherit the promises he made long ago to Jacob their ancestor. A glorious new future awaits them if they obey God's word. The advice Isaiah offers his people constitutes a Lenten agenda for us. Particularly worthy of note and reflection in our busy world is Isaiah's insistence on the importance of the Sabbath Day and its central place in Israel's life. The prophet's oracle of exhortation and promise concludes with a ringing endorsement by God himself. 'The mouth of the Lord has spoken!'

The boundless mercy and generosity of the Son of God shines through the short Gospel account of the call of Levi. Despite practising the unpopular and dubious profession of a tax-collector, Matthew was nevertheless chosen by Christ to be part of his intimate circle of friends. Christ used this occasion to reject all criticism of the kind of company he kept. The reason for his mission was to offer God's salvation to those looked upon as sinners, people on the margins of established religion. Lent reminds us that God's mercy and favour are freely available to all who approach Christ in faith, in particular those who feel distant from God.

Meditations

WEEKDAYS

FIRST WEEK OF LENT – MONDAY

Readings: Leviticus 19:1-2,11-18; Matthew 25:31-46

> *Be holy, for I, the Lord your God, am holy.*
>
> Leviticus 19:2

Both Scripture readings today perfectly complement each other. At the heart of both passages lies our duty to our neighbour. Remarkably, the book of Leviticus frames the imposition of these social demands on Israel within the context of the holiness of the Lord God himself. The community is enjoined to be holy in imitation of God who is himself holy. This injunction to be holy, far from being a purely individual and personal affair, is rather a reflection of the divine holiness and must find expression in a treatment of one's neighbour that is both just and compassionate. Leviticus here enumerates several of the Ten Commandments, but noteworthy is the insistence on a humane attitude to the afflicted, such as the dumb and the blind. The weaker members of society must be recognised as such, and not be exploited in any way. The ringing call for justice to every person, irrespective of their place in society, marks one of the outstanding contributions of the Jewish faith to the story of religion.

Moses, speaking in God's name, urged the Israelites to love their fellow-Israelite as themselves. How we are to accomplish this is spelled out for us by the Son of God in Matthew's parable of the Last Judgement scene. The hungry, the thirsty, the sick, those in prison, represent the people we are called to minister to. What is truly remarkable about Christ's teaching here is his identification with his poorer brothers and sisters. An act of kindness shown to one of these is an act of kindness done to the Son of God himself. Christ goes further by declaring that our eternal destiny will depend on the way we treat others. When the Word became flesh he became the brother of every man and woman.

FIRST WEEK OF LENT – TUESDAY

Readings: Isaiah 55:10-11; Matthew 6:7-15

*Likewise, the word which goes forth from my mouth
shall not return to me empty.*

Isaiah 55:11

The concept of God's all-powerful word has deep roots
in Scripture. Drawing a comparison from the natural
elements of rain and snow, whose ultimate effects on
the earth ensure crops and food for its inhabitants, the
prophet Isaiah states unequivocally that God's Word
will necessarily accomplish the purpose for which God
intended it. In the beginning God spoke his Word and
as a result the created order we know as the universe in
all its magnificence came into being out of nothing.
Such is the almighty power of the divine word. It was
that same Word which almighty God uttered through
his prophets, a word which communicated his saving
will and taught the people of Israel to trust in him and
believe in his promises. St John would tell us in the
prologue to his Gospel, 1:14, that the Word of God
became flesh, a human being, and made his dwelling
among us. Today's text from Isaiah finds complete
fulfilment in the incarnation of Jesus Christ.

The Gospel passage presents to us that most familiar of
all prayers, and which we know as: the Lord's Prayer.

Invested with the full authority of Christ, the Our Father has always held a privileged place in Christian piety and devotion. This prayer relates to the reading from Leviticus inasmuch as we first pray that the holiness of God's name may be everywhere recognised, and that his will may prevail in human affairs. The season of Lent brings home to us our sinfulness and consequent need of God's forgiveness. That divine forgiveness will be gladly granted, provided we extend the same pardon to those we ourselves have offended.

FIRST WEEK OF LENT – WEDNESDAY

Readings: Jonah 3:1-10; Luke 11:29-32

...the people of Nineveh repented at the preaching of Jonah

Luke 11:32

The figure of the prophet Jonah provides the link between the two Scripture readings today. The short book of Jonah tells the story of the reluctant prophet sent by God to proclaim repentance to the great pagan city of Nineveh, capital of Assyria. Despite Jonah's unwillingness, the Lord insisted that the prophet carry out his mission. The Ninevites took Jonah's message to heart, repented, and so were spared the disaster their sins would have incurred. In an Old Testament context the message of this prophetic book is remarkable. The people of Nineveh are just as precious in God's sight as his own chosen people, Israel, and their change of heart merits his favour and forbearance. God is the God of all peoples.

In the Gospel Jesus takes up the theme of the book of Jonah. Unlike the Ninevites who took seriously the words of the prophet, his own generation refused to believe him and wanted proof, a sign, of his prophetic authority. The truth was that Jesus himself in his preaching embodied a sign from God, but his hearers refused to be convinced. He refers to two well-known stories from the past, familiar to his audience. Both stories hint that Christ's message would ultimately be destined for a wider world beyond the people of Israel. The pagan unbelievers saw the light when Jonah spoke the word of God to them. The non-Israelite Queen of the South, possibly from Ethiopia, travelled far to hear the wisdom of King Solomon (1 Kings 10:1-10). If Jesus' own contemporaries could but realise it, someone greater than that famous Queen, and the prophet Jonah, stood in their midst. In this season of Lent the same Christ calls us to repentance and offers us God's salvation.

FIRST WEEK OF LENT – THURSDAY

Readings: Esther 4:17; Matthew 7:7-12

Ask, and it will be given to you.

Luke 7:7

Lent is a summons to deepen our life of prayer. The Scriptures today assure us of the power and effectiveness of heartfelt prayer, and of the wonderful truth that we have a Father in heaven who is more than willing to listen to the requests of his children. Our first reading portrays Queen Esther at prayer. Set in the Persian period of Israel's later history, the Jewish people find themselves in mortal peril. False charges have been laid against them by a wicked official of the king, and it falls to Esther to intercede with her husband to save her race from annihilation. Fearful of approaching the king, she pours her heart out to the God of her fathers, reminding him of his promises and begging for the courage and strength she so sorely needs. A fuller reading of the book shows how God heard Esther's prayer and delivered his people from danger.

Jesus Christ came to reveal the true face of God to us. The God of whom Jesus spoke is his Father and our Father, a compassionate and gracious God who cares greatly about his children. The images used by Jesus in today's Gospel passage serve to underline the goodness and concern of our God and Father. We are to be persistent and persevering in prayer and will consequently find a ready answer in heaven. If human fathers want only what is best for their children, says Jesus, how much more so our heavenly Father! Elsewhere (Lk 18:1), he exhorts us never to lose heart in prayer, and reminds his disciples (Mt 17:20), that faith can move mountains. St Augustine remarked that God always listens to our prayers, but with our eternal salvation in mind.

FIRST WEEK OF LENT– FRIDAY

Readings: Ezekiel 18: 21-28; Matthew 5:20-26

Am I to take pleasure in the death of a wicked man, says the Lord God? Instead, let him turn from his evil way and live!

Ezekiel 18:23

Upright behaviour and personal responsibility for our actions constitute the centre of our Scripture readings today. The prophet Ezekiel, who lived through the catastrophe of Israel's exile in 587 BC, reflects on how each person must ultimately be answerable before God for their moral decisions. Moses had earlier set before the nation as a whole the alternatives between life and death, a blessing or a curse (Deut 30:15-20), but now Ezekiel makes the choice between life with God and life away from God the responsibility of the individual. The blessings of the covenant will follow a life marked by justice and integrity, while unjust and immoral behaviour will necessarily alienate a person from the sphere of true life and blessing within the community of God's people. Moreover, almighty God will hold each one accountable for his actions, good or bad. Nevertheless the will of God for his people collectively and individually is one of grace and favour, what Ezekiel calls 'life'.

The gospel text is taken from what we call 'the Sermon on the Mount', and Christ's words challenge us to the very core of our feelings and actions. Anger, the source of so much ill-feeling and cause of sinfulness, must play no part in the life of the believer. The reference to the Sanhedrin betrays the Evangelist Matthew's Jewish background, but the overall thrust of Christ's teaching is clear and has wide application. Reconciliation and worship are not to be thought of as belonging to separate compartments. With good reason the Church invites us as we gather for Mass to first confess to God and before one another our sins and failings. The exchange of the sign of peace before the reception of Holy Communion reflects this particular Gospel passage. St Paul's words on Ash Wednesday make the point perfectly, '...the appeal we make in Christ's name is, 'be reconciled to God' (2 Cor 5:20).

FIRST WEEK OF LENT– SATURDAY

Readings: Deuteronomy 26:16-19; Matthew 5:43-48

Be perfect, therefore, as your heavenly Father is perfect.
Matthew 5:48

Our first reading from Deuteronomy takes us to the foundation of Israel's faith: the mystery of the covenant by which God chose this people to be his own unique possession. Almighty God has bound himself through a series of promises to confer greatness and renown on his people, surpassing that of all the other nations on earth. Through the divine favour Israel would become a nation apart, and the holiness of her way of life would be a reflection of the holiness of the Lord God himself. Moses however makes clear that the people must honour their side of the covenantal agreement. He has mediated the divine will to them in the commandments and ordinances which are to govern their life as God's people. They must ensure that they observe them. Moses' words to the people are set in the context of 'today', so underscoring the vital and timeless importance of the covenant for each new generation.

Christ raises the teaching of Moses to a new level in his interpretation of the command to love one's neighbour. The language used leaves little room for doubt or discussion. In imitation of our heavenly Father, our love and concern for others must know no bounds. The Creator of heaven and earth permits his sun to shine and give warmth and nurture to good and bad alike, and likewise with life-giving rainfall. His generosity and munificence make no distinction. The Son of God stipulates that it is to be the same with his disciples. The whole of the New Testament is unanimous that the essence of what Christ taught can be summed up in love of God and love of neighbour. He has made us part of the new covenant with God his Father. Our commitment to that covenant finds expression in a generous love for all human beings without exception. In that way we will be aspiring to the perfection of the Father himself.

SECOND WEEK OF LENT – MONDAY

Readings: Daniel 9:4-10; Luke 6:36-38

Give, and it will be given to you.

Luke 6:38

The communal penitential dimension of Lent is well expressed in this extract from the book of Daniel. Perhaps we in our time need to rediscover the importance and deep significance of a communal act of penance in our life together as God's people. The large crowds who assemble to receive ashes on Ash Wednesday suggest a communal awareness of solidarity in penance. The prophet Daniel laments publicly before God the sins and faults of his people. By departing from God's way they have been scattered among the nations. Of themselves, they can only hang their heads in shame, but nevertheless recognise that they can still invoke God whose love is tender and whose nature is compassionate. Daniel's sincere and frank acknowledgement that the words and warnings of God's prophets have gone unheeded allows his people to let go of their sinful past, receive the divine mercy and so recover the joy of life as God's chosen people.

Penance for the Christian must bring about new horizons within us. Jesus has revealed the face of the Father to us, a God who is all-compassion and who desires his children to display that compassion to one another. The teaching of Jesus gets to the very roots of our motives and manner of behaviour. We are not to sit in judgement on others, and if we wish to receive God's forgiveness we must be prepared to forgive others. Christ is here assuring us that to embark on the path of generosity and pardon will bring us blessings in abundance. Part of the Lenten call is to tear down the walls of our own often self-enclosed world, and to open ourselves to the healing balm of Christ's words. He waits to give a full and overflowing measure to us.

SECOND WEEK OF LENT – TUESDAY

Readings: Isaiah 1:10,16-20; Matthew 23:1-12

The greatest among you must be your servant.
Matthew 23:11

The prophets of Israel used forthright language in their denunciation of sin and injustice. Isaiah provides a classic example of this plain speaking when he addresses the governing classes as 'rulers of Sodom', and the nation as 'people of Gomorrah'. These cities had become by-words for wickedness and corruption (Gen cc 18-20), and the prophet's choice of such terms indicates just how low the nation had sunk in religious and moral terms. Notwithstanding severe strictures such as these on the part of the prophets, they nevertheless proclaimed that the door to repentance and God's mercy always remained open. A change of heart, manifested in integrity of life and concern for others, would ensure that God would no longer hold them to account for their past sins. Isaiah's recourse to the vivid imagery of 'colour opposites' – scarlet/white as snow, red/white as wool – serves to underline the extent of the divine forgiveness.

Both the text of Isaiah and that of our Gospel have particular application for those placed in authority, and for all who hold positions of responsibility. Christ, with the civil and religious leaders of his day in mind, states in words reminiscent of Ash Wednesday's Gospel that vain outward show in matters of piety counts for nothing before God. Such selfish behaviour and wilful disregard for others amounts to hypocrisy. Christ has come to establish a new order of values, one in which all social distinctions and rank become relative. He teaches that God is our Father and each person is precious before him. Christ himself is the only real teacher of wisdom. If anyone aspires to true Christian greatness this must mean being at the service of others. That was a lesson insisted upon by Christ, and one which he supremely exemplified by his own life of service which ultimately led him to the cross.

SECOND WEEK OF LENT – WEDNESDAY

Readings: Jeremiah 18:18-20; Matthew 20:17-28

The Son of Man came not to be served, but to serve.

Matthew 20:28

The trials and tribulations of the seventh century BC prophet, Jeremiah, have been seen as foreshadowing those of the Son of God himself. In their mission of proclaiming the Word of God to Israel, the prophets regularly encountered indifference, misunderstanding, and even rejection. The time of national crisis in which Jeremiah lived was one of suspicion and danger, and it was a crisis that would end in the destruction of Jerusalem and exile to Babylon for the chosen people. The prophet endeavoured to offer an explanation for this critical situation and at the same time give a word of hope as a way forward for the nation. The innocent Jeremiah in this passage laments before God the plots against his life that are being hatched against him by his enemies, despite the fact that he often interceded on their behalf. Innocent suffering often characterised the lives of God's servants.

From what we read in the Gospels, Jesus Christ himself lived under the shadow of threat and suffering. In today's Gospel he is at pains to explain to his disciples the humiliation and death by crucifixion that ultimately awaited him, but adding that he would rise again after three days. The Evangelist Matthew then appends the story of the brothers James and John with their mother's request that they be given first seats in Jesus' kingdom. This provides Jesus with the opportunity to give a pointed lesson on what honour and service might mean in the new order he has come to inaugurate. The way of the rulers of the world is far removed from what he has in mind. Greatness deserving of the name must be rooted in the service of one's fellow disciples. Paradoxically, that person will be ranked first who puts the interests of others before his own. The striking self-description of Jesus says it all: *The Son of Man came not to be served, but to serve, and to offer his life as a ransom for many.*

SECOND WEEK OF LENT – THURSDAY

Readings: Jeremiah 17:5-10; Luke 16:19-31

Blessed is the man who places his trust in the Lord
                                                    Jeremiah 17:7

Sacred Scripture stands as the supreme witness to the mind of God and to the gradual revelation of his plan for the salvation and well-being of the people of Israel. Prophets, such as Jeremiah, were the great exponents and interpreters of that plan. In language reminiscent of the first Psalm, and drawing on the teaching of Moses (Deut c28), the prophet Jeremiah muses on the two choices that lie before mankind. That person has lost his way who deliberately excludes God from his manner of life and aspires to be self-sufficient, relying instead on all that is mortal and on what the ephemeral world has to offer. Jeremiah describes such an existence as being barren and accursed, because God plays no part in it. On the other hand, to place one's confidence in God and make him the centre of one's life will ensure happiness and bring blessing. Employing pastoral imagery, the prophet describes the pious person as being like a deeply rooted tree which flourishes and bears fruit in spite of arid conditions. The season of Lent, and Jeremiah's words, remind us of the serious choices we have to make.

The Gospel parable of the rich man and Lazarus highlights the vital importance of those decisions we take which affect our neighbour. The parable of Jesus leaves little room for comfort, because our eternal destiny rests on the responsible way in which we use God's gifts. In some sense our poor neighbour lies at our gate everyday, even if not literally, usually in the person of those we live with or encounter in the course of a day. The rich man went to eternal punishment for failing to share his good things with someone less well off than himself, and only realised his mistake when it was too late. Having made his choices, he now found himself excluded from God's presence forever. Lent provides us with a God-given opportunity to re-examine our priorities in life and, if necessary, make changes. We are called by God to choose life and a blessing.

SECOND WEEK OF LENT – FRIDAY

Readings: Genesis 37:3-4,12-13,17-28;
Matthew 21:33-43,45-46

Now Israel loved Joseph more than his other sons.

Genesis 37:3

We hear from the book of Genesis today how Joseph, the youngest and favourite son of the patriarch Jacob, was resented by his brothers, and was sold out of jealousy as a captive and taken to Egypt. The story of Joseph is a very human story, charged with emotion, and shot through with pain and suffering, not least on the part of his aged father. It is also a sacred narrative in which the guiding hand of God, though invisible, is unerringly at work. What appears to be the tragic fate of Joseph resulting from jealousy and betrayal by his brothers, would turn out to be a story of redemption. Divine providence ensured that Joseph prospered in the land of Egypt, and he would prove to be the saviour of his family by delivering them from the famine that afflicted their own land of Canaan. With the fuller understanding of faith, the Church sees the figure of Christ and his sufferings foreshadowed in Joseph's travails. Through the wonder and inscrutability of God's power, like Joseph, the crucified Christ would become the saviour not only of his own people, but of the whole world.

The Gospel parable of the vineyard and the wicked tenants likewise speaks of violence and rejection. The parable may possibly be read as a reflection of the fractured history of God's people, Israel. Isaiah, for example, depicts Israel as the vineyard of the Lord (Isa 5:1-7), a choice plantation on which Almighty God lavished every possible care, only to be rewarded with a harvest of bitter grapes. The harsh treatment meted out on occasion to God's prophets resembles that received by the messengers in the parable, while the ultimate fate of the owner's son can only be a thinly veiled allusion to the Passion and death of Jesus Christ himself. Yet from the tragedy of Christ's rejection and crucifixion God made salvation possible for the gentile world. The Evangelist Matthew reflects the amazement and marvel of the early Church at God's ways revealed in Christ by appending the text of the Psalm: *The stone which the builders rejected has become the cornerstone. This is the work of the Lord and it is marvellous in our eyes* (Ps 118, vv 22-23).

SECOND WEEK OF LENT – SATURDAY

Readings: Micah 7:14-15,18-20; Luke 15:1-3,11-32

*It is only right that we should rejoice. Your brother was
dead and has returned to life; He was lost and has been
found.*

Luke 15:32

The prophets of Israel in their prayers never tired of
reminding God of his great mercies of old and the
wonders he accomplished for them long ago, usually
with reference to the Exodus from Egypt, the greatest
and most definitive of all God's saving acts on behalf of
his people Israel. There is an evocative, even poignant
strain to the words of the eighth century BC prophet
Micah, in today's reading. Micah yearns for times past,
when the Lord showed himself to be the true shepherd
of his people. The prophet now calls upon God to
remember his compassionate and forgiving nature, and
to take away the burden of Israel's sins, consigning
them to the depths of the sea. He prays that his people
may once more experience that same fidelity and love
which the God of Israel originally manifested to their
fathers.

The prophetic portrait of a merciful and compassionate
God is elevated to an altogether different level in the
magnificent parable of the prodigal son. This parable

depicting an infinitely loving God and Father was the response of Jesus to those who accused him of associating with disreputable company. The extent of the father's forgiveness towards his wayward son borders on the reckless in human terms. The unreserved welcome the selfish son received despite the fact that he led a wilful and profligate life, along with the subsequent feast laid on in his honour, are details intended to underline the unbelievable extent of the divine forgiveness towards those who consider themselves least worthy of it. The Son of God has in truth come to seek out and to save those who were lost. This quest of Christ embodies the true meaning of Lent which, irrespective of our guilt and sin, means coming back home to God our Father where our true interests lie, and where an unimaginable welcome awaits us.

THIRD WEEK OF LENT– MONDAY

Readings: 2 Kings 5:1-15; Luke 4:24-30

But passing through their midst he went on his way.
Luke 4:30

Both Lenten readings today invite us to reflect on the mysterious gift of faith in Christ which we are privileged to enjoy. In her fuller understanding of Sacred Scripture, the Church sees in the healing of Naaman the Syrian by the eighth century prophet Elisha a foreshadowing and anticipation of the preaching of the Gospel to the gentile world. Naaman who was afflicted with leprosy, after some reluctance, agreed to bathe in the river Jordan and was healed through the word of the prophet. The story hints at the possibility of non-Israelites coming to faith in the God of Israel, acknowledged now by Naaman as the God of all the earth. We are also reminded of how the people of Israel were the first to receive the revelation of God. In the words of St Paul, *it was they who received adoption, the glory, and the covenants; to them was entrusted the Law, the worship, and the promises. To them belong the Fathers, and from them Christ was born according to the flesh* (Rom 9:4-5). The Church will be forever indebted to the Jewish people for their fidelity to God's revelation. Through them we are heirs of the new covenant.

The rejection which Christ experienced from the people of Nazareth causes him to hark back to the healing of Naaman, and to the encounter of Elijah with the widow from the town of Zarephath, (1 Kings 17:7-16). Both prophets, in God's design, ministered to those who did not belong to the chosen people. Jesus was issuing a scarcely veiled warning to his own townspeople of Nazareth that their obstinacy and refusal to believe in him would have implications similar to those in the days of Elijah and his disciple Elisha. Israel's unique status as God's people must always leave them open to the mystery of God's wider plan. Christ, the greatest of prophets, stood in their midst and they failed to recognise him. Similarly, God can and wishes to use our faith in Christ to reach out to a wider world. One of the graces of Lent is for us to recognise the responsibility that the gift of faith entails.

THIRD WEEK OF LENT – TUESDAY

Readings: Daniel 3:25, 34-43; Matthew 18:21-35

So will my heavenly Father do to you, unless you each forgive your brother from your heart.

Matthew 18:35

Forgiveness was central to the teaching of Christ. Those who wanted to be part of the Kingdom of God which he proclaimed must be people animated with the spirit of forgiveness. The Evangelists and the other New Testament writers affirm that love of our neighbour expressed in forgiveness lay at the very heart of Christ's Gospel. The simplicity and clarity of our Gospel parable today should not blind us to the profound implications of the lesson it conveys. As the story goes, the first servant was unable repay the huge debt he owed to his master. Moved by compassion, his master generously refrained from punishing him and granted him time to mend his ways. Despite being the recipient of such kindness himself, the servant refused to behave in the same way towards his fellow-servant who stood indebted to him for a very small sum. The punishment originally threatened on the first servant was now inevitable. We discern in this parable a reflection of our relationship to almighty God and to others. God does not hold our offences against us, but is ever ready and willing to grant us pardon. The Son of God, however, consistently warns us that this divine forgiveness remains contingent upon our willingness to forgive others.

The extract from the book of Daniel is a fine example of Israel in penitential mode before God, and eminently suitable for a Lenten liturgy. Azariah, just delivered from the fiery furnace, prays to God for his people who are sorely reduced. He calls upon God to remember his ancient promises to their fathers and to look with mercy upon them in their present predicament. Scattered among the nations and deprived of their place of worship, they are turning to God with humble and contrite hearts, asking for his mercy and favour. Reading this text of Daniel in the light of today's Gospel, we discover that this mercy and pardon will be forthcoming from God, provided we in like manner extend to our neighbour mercy and pardon as well.

THIRD WEEK OF LENT – WEDNESDAY

Readings: Deuteronomy 4:1,5-9; Matthew 5:17-19

Do not think that I have come to abolish the Law or the Prophets. I have not come to abolish them, but to fulfil them.

Matthew 5:17

The saving plan of God for the world, first hinted at in the call of Abraham and gradually unfolded over many centuries through the prophets and wisdom teachers of Israel, reached perfection in Jesus Christ. The words of Jesus in today's gospel leave us in no doubt that the great body of writings we know as the Old Testament receive their definitive fulfilment in him. Christ, therefore, is the supreme interpreter of the Law of Moses and of the prophetic oracles. The reason he can give them their definitive meaning is because he is the Son of God, ever with the Father, and so being God was active throughout the long history of Israel. The Church today urges us to rediscover the presence and power of God's word enshrined in the Old Testament, and to read this account of God's ways against the fuller light of the New Testament. The early Church struggled to understand fully the unity of both Testaments, but never doubted that in Jesus Christ was to be found the key to all Scripture.

In our reading from Deuteronomy, Moses lays before Israel the wonder and privilege that is their inheritance as God's people. No other nation can claim to have such an intimacy with their god as that enjoyed by Israel with the Lord God. The laws and statutes given them by God embody a wisdom that is the envy of the rest of the world. In these laws are to be found the will of God for his chosen people, and Moses solemnly enjoins Israel to keep and observe them, and pass them on to future generations. As we ponder these Lenten readings with their emphasis on teaching, we recall our own obligations as the baptised people of God to teach and hand on the faith in all its fullness to our children and young people. We have a rich inheritance that the next generation deserves to share.

THIRD WEEK OF LENT – THURSDAY

Readings: Jeremiah 7:23-28; Luke 11:14-23

*But if it is by the finger of God that I cast out devils,
then indeed the Kingdom of God has come among you.*

Luke 14:20

Both our Scripture readings today emerge from settings
of controversy and opposition. In his celebrated
discourse at the gates of the Jerusalem Temple (c 7), the
prophet Jeremiah bitterly laments the failure of God's
people to follow the way God marked out for them.
Such backsliding, the prophet says, has characterised
the whole history of Israel from the time they came
out of the land of Egypt. The wider context of this
chapter describes Jeremiah denouncing the hypocritical
worship that takes place in the Temple, and the
underlying false presumption that God would never
allow the Temple to be destroyed. The insincerity of
their prayers and sacrifices is reflected in their stubborn
and godless behaviour. The divine disappointment is
acute. God had expected better from his people.

In the Gospel, Christ is forced to defend himself from
the appalling charge of being in league with the devil.
His power over the evil spirits was alleged to have
come from the prince of devils. Christ's accusers failed
to rise above their prejudices and perceive the

significance of his healing works. In some obscure way
Satan was believed to hold sway over the world, and it
was this stranglehold which Christ came to break. If his
opponents could only recognise the demonstration of
God's power which was taking place before their very
eyes, then they would realise that the long-awaited
Kingdom of God had now arrived in their midst. Both
Jeremiah's hearers and Christ's contemporaries rejected
the moment of God's grace and the time of salvation.
In the liturgical 'now' of Lent, God continues to speak
to us through the words of the prophets, and above all
through the Word Incarnate, Jesus Christ, his Son. We
must exercise our responsibility and listen, and then we
must act on what we hear.

THIRD WEEK OF LENT – FRIDAY

Readings: Hosea 14:2-10; Mark 12:28-34

You must love the Lord your God with all your heart...
You must love your neighbour as yourself. No
commandment is greater than these.

Mark 12:30-31

The final verses of the book of Hosea conclude with an appeal to Israel to return to the Lord God, to the only one able to safeguard the nation's true interests. All other avenues lead to disappointment and disillusion because, being merely human devices, they represent attempts to act independently of God. The prophet points out how past reliance on other nations has failed to deliver the people from danger, while idolatrous worship has only provoked the wrath of God. True conversion, which the prophets call 'returning to the Lord', will allay the divine anger and ensure a brighter future for God's people. Despite the angry and apparently fiery preaching of Hosea, his image of God is a tender one, a God who loves and cherishes his bride, Israel. God's plans are plans for salvation and blessing, and in the end his love will prevail. Prophetic words such as these help prepare the way for the supreme expression of God's love in the fullness of time which was revealed in his own Son, his eternal Word, who took up his dwelling among us.

Jesus Christ came to us as the great teacher of humanity. His insistence that the foremost commandments are love of God and love of neighbour takes us to the very core of true religion. Lent is a time for returning to the basics of our faith, and this short Gospel can serve both as an examination of conscience and a yardstick of true spiritual progress. Christ revolutionised our relationship with God and with our fellow human beings, but at the same time he magisterially simplified these relationships. We stand justified in God's eyes if we bear one another's burdens for the love of God. By placing the interests of others before our own we are putting on the mind of Christ (Phil 2:5), which is the whole purpose of our Christian existence.

THIRD WEEK OF LENT – SATURDAY

Readings: Hosea 5:16-6:6; Luke 18:9-14

Your devotion is like a morning cloud, like the dew which quickly vanishes.

Hosea 5:4

The words of Hosea read for us in today's liturgy suggest a repentance on the part of Israel which is shallow and fleeting, aptly compared by the prophet to a morning cloud or early dew which does not last. The naïve presumption that God will always be at hand to rescue also comes in for criticism. Almighty God's frustration and bewilderment at his people's arrogance is powerfully depicted by Hosea. We encounter here the mystery of God's involvement with his chosen people Israel, and the apparent pain and distress at their failure to measure up to their part of the covenant which he sealed with them on Mount Sinai. In remarkable language, God speaks of cutting his people to pieces by the words of the prophets in an attempt to win them back to himself. Their whole ritual of sacrifice and worship was merely external and superficial. True piety and knowledge of God's will were found to be sadly lacking.

The familiar Gospel parable of the Pharisee and the tax collector with its somewhat surprising conclusion teaches that human beings may never boast before God.

In both his letters to the Corinthians and that to the Romans, the apostle Paul returns frequently to the theme that any accomplishment or achievement we can claim is entirely due to God's mercy and grace, given to us in Christ. The Pharisee of the parable was undoubtedly a good man, but his pride and excessive self-esteem, coupled with his disdain for the tax collector, failed to find favour in God's sight. Lent sheds God's light on the dark areas of our life. If we wish to find our true worth before God then we need to be humble and not pass judgement on others.

FOURTH WEEK OF LENT – MONDAY

Readings: Isaiah 65:17-21; John 4:43-54

And he believed, and his whole household with him.
John 4:53

Our reading today from the prophet Isaiah offers us an attractive, even homely, vision of the future God has in store for his people. The prophet looks beyond the shortcomings and limitations of the present life, and dares to speak of a new heaven and a new earth which the Lord God plans to create. The imagery employed in this picture of the future is naturally very much rooted in this world, in a language intelligible to the prophet's contemporaries. Yet Isaiah is proclaiming God's desire to transform the fortunes of Israel for the better, and as the Creator of the world he has the power to change sorrow and tears into joy and gladness. With their rock-like faith in God's saving design, the prophets strained towards a future and a description of an entirely new order of creation, vastly different from the world as we know it. God's fidelity was never in question, and this new order would without doubt come to pass at his chosen time.

The miracles of Jesus Christ afford us a glimpse of the divine power in action on earth. They also teach us of God's care for those afflicted with sickness and human ills. The future envisaged by Isaiah, marked by an absence of sadness and tears, began to take shape in the healing ministry of the Lord Jesus. In response to the father's urgent pleas, grounded in a deep faith in the power of Christ to save, the word of Jesus was sufficient to heal the official's son as today's Gospel relates. Christ's miracles still stand as an invitation to us to turn to him, the healer of body and soul, who continues to be present and active in the life of his Church, especially through her sacramental ministry. Lent calls us to a renewal of faith, to an ever deeper appreciation that the Son of God remains with us in all his power until the end of time. He is the living expression of God's fidelity.

FOURTH WEEK OF LENT – TUESDAY

Readings: Ezekiel 47:1-9; John 5:1-3, 5-16

...the trees will bear new fruit every month because these waters flow from the sanctuary...

Ezekiel 47:12

The book of Ezekiel concludes (cc 40-48), with the prophet's splendid vision of the future new Temple. The picture is an idealistic one, envisaging a return to the fruitful conditions of Eden because of the life-giving waters which flow from the sanctuary of the Temple. In other words, the waters have their source in God who will wonderfully bestow new life on his people and their land when the Temple and the holy city are restored. In his magnificent and detailed picture Ezekiel is looking beyond the situation of his time, marked by destruction, dispersal and exile, to a glorious new dispensation which the Lord God has in store for his people. The central place which the new Temple will occupy denotes the coming presence and dwelling of God in the midst of his people. The prophet's dream remains a lofty and inspiring one.

The theme of water links the Gospel of the day with the passage from Ezekiel. The paralysed man was unable to reach the healing waters at Bethzatha in order to be healed, but with Jesus Christ something greater than these waters was present: the Son of God himself. By his healing word he demonstrated his divine, life-giving power which was uniquely his as the Son of the Father. The fourth Evangelist, John, seems to have had the text of Ezekiel in mind, (Jn 19:34-35) when he describes the piercing of the crucified Christ's side and the resultant flow of blood and water, symbolising the sacraments of the Eucharist and Baptism from which the Church draws her life. Through the sacramental ministry of the Church, Christ continues to dispense his divine and life-giving power to us who believe from the altar and the sanctuary. Part of our Lenten discipline is for us to appreciate that the grandeur of Ezekiel's vision of the waters of life has now become a reality in the ongoing redemptive work of Jesus Christ, continually mediated to us through the Church he founded.

FOURTH WEEK OF LENT – WEDNESDAY

Readings: Isaiah 49:8-15; John 5:17-30

I do not seek to do my own will, but the will of him who sent me.

John 5:30

The prophet Isaiah in the first reading today addresses a word of comfort and reassurance to a people beaten and bowed by suffering, and who had furthermore endured the pain of being exiled from their own land. Far from forgetting them, the God and Lord of history will ensure their triumphant homecoming through a landscape transformed for their benefit. In majestic tones, Isaiah calls upon the heavens and the earth to rejoice at the restoration of Israel's fortunes. God would once more demonstrate his almighty power and his unswerving will to save. Invoking the tender image of mother and child, the prophet declares that even if in the unlikely event a mother would abandon the child of her womb, the nature of God's attachment to Israel is such that he could never forsake her. The fluctuating tide and fortunes of human events are unable to alter or frustrate the divine purpose, because God remains the sovereign Lord of all history.

The Gospel story presents us with Jesus' explanation of why he has the authority to heal a paralytic on the

Sabbath. Hinting at what would later form part of the Church's teaching on the Holy Trinity, Jesus claims to be acting and working solely on his Father's behalf. There is complete unity of purpose between himself and his Father. He is endowed with the full authority of the Father on earth, and to dishonour him is to dishonour the Father himself. Through his miracles and teaching he gives life here and now to those physically and spiritually afflicted, and when the time comes as Son of Man he will also summon forth the dead to resurrection and judgement. As Jesus himself explained it, his union with God his Father is so intimate that he enjoys equality of status with him. Our Gospel passage opens with the resentment of his opponents who realised the enormity of his claim as Son of God.

FOURTH WEEK OF LENT – THURSDAY

Readings: Exodus 32:7-14; John 5:31-47

My testimony surpasses that of John.

John 5:36

Our opening reading from Exodus demonstrates the powerful effectiveness of intercessory prayer before God. While Moses was on Mount Sinai in communion with God the Israelites became restless and made for themselves an idol in the form of a golden calf. Their idolatrous behaviour was an outrage to God and, the account says, he thereupon resolved to finish and be done with them. As a mediator, Moses stood in the breach and pleaded with God in very human terms. Was the wonder of the Exodus to count for nothing? He reminded God of his long-standing promises to their fathers of a land of their own and countless offspring. Moses' plea, we are told, placated God, and he refrained from giving way to his fierce anger. The Gospel on Ash Wednesday highlighted prayer as one of the three great exercises of Lent. As the episode of the gold calf powerfully demonstrates, the act of intercessory prayer on behalf of others finds favour before God. Such prayer is both an effective and a worthy Lenten discipline.

The later part of Lent, liturgically speaking, corresponds to the latter stages of Christ's earthly ministry, especially as related in John's Gospel. The fourth Evangelist in our Gospel presents Jesus summoning witnesses in his defence as Son of the Father, in what could almost be described as a form of trial or legal setting. The witnesses that Jesus invokes are John the Baptist, his own miracles, Moses, and the Scriptures themselves. Each of these in their own way provides clear and unique testimony that Jesus is the one sent by the Father, the bearer of God's truth to the world. However, their self-centred and prejudiced attitude hinders his adversaries from seeing in Christ the Messiah and Saviour long promised by God to their nation. We pray on this day of Lent for the grace to grow ever more in the knowledge of God our Father, and of Jesus Christ, the one he has anointed and sent into this world.

FOURTH WEEK OF LENT – FRIDAY

Readings: Wisdom 2:1,12-22; John 7:1-2,10,25-30

Let us lie in wait for the just man, for he is burdensome to us.

Wisdom 2:12

As the season of Passiontide approaches, the Church applies to Christ the theme of the just man's sufferings as expounded in the Book of Wisdom. The pious Jew, by his upright and godly way of life, was an object of ridicule and reproach to a pagan world. To be faithful to God's law and commandments invited condemnation, even persecution. In the midst of such a hostile environment, the faith of the just man remains unflinching. He knows that his trust in God will not be misplaced, and that his tenacity and piety will ultimately be rewarded. As we contemplate Christ's sufferings, we can draw inspiration and encouragement from these words of Wisdom in our own struggle to lead the Christian life. Almighty God will never desert those who remain faithful to him.

The Gospel tells us that on the occasion of the feast of Tabernacles, which recalled Israel's sojourn in the wilderness, the words of Jesus cause a division within the crowd listening to him. In a passage replete with irony, his audience asserted that they knew who exactly

Jesus was, and where he came from. They were of course mistaken. Jesus alone could speak of his origins, because they lay in eternity with his Father. Only he could in truth claim to know the Father. By concentrating on Christ's earthly background they closed their minds to the possibility that God's Son was standing in their midst and speaking from the Temple, the dwelling-place of his Father. In a sombre connection with our Wisdom reading, we hear that the crowd would have laid hands on him, but the hour when God would permit this had not yet arrived. The 'hour' of Jesus is mentioned on a number of occasions in John's Gospel and refers to the glorification of Jesus that will result through his death and Resurrection (Jn 17:1). It is an hour that the Father alone will determine, and at a time of his choosing.

FOURTH WEEK OF LENT – SATURDAY

Readings: Jeremiah 11:18-20; John 7:40-52

But I was like an innocent lamb being led to the slaughter.

Jeremiah 11:18

Of all the prophets who proclaimed God's Word to Israel, none suffered more than Jeremiah. His life of trial and tribulation foreshadows the fate of Jesus Christ himself. Employing a deeply symbolic image from the religious language of the nation, Jeremiah compares himself to an innocent lamb being taken to the slaughter-house. It was the blood of the Paschal lamb smeared on the doorposts that saved the Israelites from death in Egypt (Ex 12:1-14). Later, John the Baptist would point out Jesus as the Lamb of God who takes away the sins of the world (Jn 1:29). All of Scripture points to Christ and finds its fulfilment in him. The intrigues and plots devised against Jeremiah as he brought the Word of God to his people mirror the actions and behaviour of Jesus' own disbelieving con-temporaries in their obstinacy and defiance. The short reading from Jeremiah concludes with a ringing cry of trust in God, which brings to mind the unshakeable confidence of Christ in his Father's will.

A recurrent theme in the Fourth Gospel is the division and disagreement that Jesus causes among the crowd, including the religious leaders. Some wanted to believe in him as the prophet Moses promised that God would one day raise up. Some surmised he might even be the Lord's anointed One. Others in ignorance refused to believe in him. The Temple police, sent to arrest him, found themselves overwhelmed by the power of his words. The religious authorities, the Pharisees, declared solemnly that prophets do not come from Galilee. Their misguided certainty and self-assurance blinded them to the possibility that God could be speaking and active in the person and words of the one present among them, Jesus Christ. Rather than face this possibility, they preferred to arrest him. The acceptable time, God's moment of salvation, would pass them by.

FIFTH WEEK OF LENT – MONDAY

Readings: Daniel 13:1-9,15-17,19-30,33-62;
John 8:12-20

*I am the light of the world. Anyone who follows me
will not be walking in darkness, but will have the light
of life.*

John 8:12

The Church in her Lenten liturgy employs a wide
variety of Scriptural texts, all of which are intended to
shed light on the person of Jesus Christ who is the key
to the whole of Scripture. We read today in the book
of Daniel how the innocent Susanna was saved from
false accusers and an unjust death through the wisdom
and integrity of the young man, Daniel. As the days of
the Lord's Passion and death approach, the story of
Susanna reminds us of the innocent Christ, who was
also falsely accused and subjected to a cruel death on
the cross. Christ too would be vindicated and declared
innocent through the power of the Father who raised
him from the dead and revealed him as the Lord of
glory. We can sometimes feel that our personal sufferings
and trials, often unlooked for, pass unnoticed. The
Susanna episode teaches that in the end divine justice
will prevail and God will hear and answer our cry for
vindication.

In a setting of confrontation with the Pharisees and others who disputed his exalted claims, Jesus declares in our Gospel passage that he is the light of the world, and all who follow him will find true enlightenment through his teaching. The light he refers to is none other than the teaching he brings into this world from another sphere, the divine sphere of God his Father. A notable feature of John's Gospel is the use the Evangelist makes of natural elements to convey the true identity of Jesus and what it is he offers. In the Fourth Gospel Jesus describes himself as the bread of life, the giver of living water, the true vine, and even life itself (c 11). The horizons of those who bitterly contested Christ's words were human and therefore necessarily limited. His authority to teach and be the true light of the world derives from the fact that he came forth from God the Father and would return to him. His knowledge and understanding belong to an altogether different order. Lent is an ongoing invitation to us to walk in the light of the Lord and then, in the light of Christ's truth, we can gain a sense of true direction.

FIFTH WEEK OF LENT – TUESDAY

Readings: Numbers 21:4-9; John 8:21-30

When you have lifted up the Son of Man, then you will know that I am He.

John 8:28

The Book of Numbers recounts how the Israelites during their wilderness wanderings murmured against God and Moses and were consequently punished by fiery serpents. In his mercy God provided them with a means of healing through a bronze serpent raised high. By fixing their gaze on this bronze serpent they were cured of their affliction. The Evangelist John sees the crucified Christ foreshadowed in this incident of the bronze serpent. Several times in his Gospel John speaks of Jesus being 'raised up', as he does in today's passage (8:28), and this 'lifting up' would be a moment when the truth about Jesus would be fully revealed to the world. John chooses his language carefully, and does not separate the cross of Jesus from his glorification. In John's theological outlook, the cross and death of Christ formed a part of a single event, and were but a prelude to the revelation of his true glory as the Son of God disclosed in his Resurrection from the dead.

The increasingly contentious debate between Jesus and his audience is evident from our Gospel passage. His adversaries are unable to understand him, or know where he comes from, because their mindset is that of the flesh which prevents them from acknowledging the truth. When they have 'raised up' Jesus then the complete truth about his divine identity would be revealed, because it would all be the work of his heavenly Father, something they are unable to grasp. Christ on the cross is central to our Catholic faith and devotion. The Lenten liturgy of this day invites us to look at the One lifted up on the cross, ponder on what we see, and find there the most compelling evidence and expression of God's love for us. As the Israelites in the desert once found relief through gazing at the bronze serpent, we too shall find healing and new life by fixing our gaze on Christ crucified.

FIFTH WEEK OF LENT – WEDNESDAY

Readings: Daniel 3:14-20,24-25,28; John 8:31-42

If you remain in my word you will indeed be my disciples. You will know the truth, and the truth will set you free.

John 8:31-2

Our liturgy opens today with the well-known story of Daniel and his companions, thrown into the blazing furnace because of their refusal to worship the image of a god. The second Commandment expressly forbade such worship, so rather than disobey God's law the young men were prepared to face an excruciating death. The aim of this story, with its background of persecution of the Jewish people, is to encourage perseverance and faith in God who remains faithful to his covenant and will never abandon those who trust in him. As the deliverance of Daniel and his friends eloquently illustrates, the greater the danger and the intensity of persecution so much the greater is the power of God to deliver his chosen ones. This same trust in God would also sustain Jesus in his bitter struggle with those who opposed his mission and had evil designs on his life.

The closely argued and sharp debate that characterises the eighth chapter of John's Gospel increases in intensity, with Christ's assertion to his hearers that as the Son of the Father he is able to set the children of Abraham free. Their obstinate and increasingly belligerent attitude to Jesus betrays their claim to be genuine descendants of the Patriarch. Their sinfulness has enslaved them and prevents them from recognising him who is the true and rightful heir in God's house. Jesus stands firmly by his insistence that he has come from the God they claim to worship. If they remained consistent to the faith of Abraham, Christ's words would find an echo within them, and they would love the Son in the same way that they declare they love God their Father. There are tragic overtones to this passage as the rejection of Jesus by his own generation becomes ever more evident. The truth of God, the Incarnate Word in person, stood in their midst, yet such is the obduracy of the human heart that they preferred not to believe that he is the fulfilment of the faith which has its origins in God's call to Abraham. Let us open our hearts to the fullness of God's truth revealed to us in Jesus Christ, a truth which is kept ever fresh in the memory of the Church.

FIFTH WEEK OF LENT – THURSDAY

Readings: Genesis 17:3-9; John 8:51-59

I will make you the father of a multitude of nations.
Genesis 17:5

The Patriarch Abraham forms a bond between both Scripture readings today. In Genesis we hear Almighty God reaffirming his covenant with Abraham and his descendants, promising that he would be their God from one generation to the next. The change in the Patriarch's name from Abram to Abraham gives a universal note to his role in God's plan for the human race. God has destined him to become the father in faith of numerous nations. The dispersal of humanity through pride and sin as recounted in the early section of Genesis (see ch.9) would be reversed in the offspring of Abraham. Much later, the apostle Paul in his reflection on this text identified the seed of Abraham with Jesus Christ (Gal 3:16). God's covenant is one of divine graciousness and favour, quite unmerited on the part of any human being, and an expression of his enduring fidelity. The covenant which began with Abraham points towards the new and everlasting covenant between God and the whole human family, sealed in the blood of Jesus Christ.

As chapter eight of John's Gospel draws to a conclusion the drama intensifies. Jesus promises eternal life to those who hear and accept his word, an assertion which infuriates his listeners because it implies a status that transcends what is human. In a scene reminiscent of a courtroom setting, his adversaries accuse Jesus of being superior to Abraham and those towering figures of Israel's history, the prophets. They demand an answer as to who exactly Jesus is claiming to be. Once more Jesus states that his mission is incomprehensible without reference to God his Father, whose glory alone he seeks, and of whom he as Son possesses an intimate knowledge. His life's work on earth is one of faithful obedience to his Father, with whom he dwelt even before the time of Abraham. The attempt on his life by stoning on the part of his outraged adversaries clearly presages his forthcoming trial and death sentence.

FIFTH WEEK OF LENT – FRIDAY

Readings: Jeremiah 20:10-13; John 10:31-42

You will know and understand that the Father is in me, and I am in the Father.

John 10:38

In today's first reading, the prophet Jeremiah lays bares his soul before God, and we hear him complain about the plots and intrigue his enemies are devising against him. Surrounded by such adversity, however, his faith in God does not waver. The human heart with all its motives lies open before God, and he will uphold the righteousness of Jeremiah's cause in the face of such great hostility. With the approach of Holy Week, the sufferings and travail of Jeremiah, prophet and man of God, inevitably bring to mind Christ's own Passion. With the eye of faith, we can see in Jeremiah's steadfast faith and refusal to yield to his hostile opponents, a prophetic image of the future Messiah promised to Israel. Through the upheavals and pain of the prophet's life, almighty God, the divine teacher, was preparing us for the even greater drama of his own Son's sufferings, death and Resurrection.

As John's Gospel unfolds, the grounds for the hostility against Jesus become ever clearer. The accusation laid against him is that of blasphemy. He is only human, yet by his words he is placing himself on a level that is divine, and so making himself equal to God. Central to the fourth Evangelist's technique is that Christ's accusers actually speak the truth about Jesus, although unaware that they are doing so. In their ignorance and malice they are confessing who he really is. Jesus continues to insist, in his own defence, that he is carrying out the work of his Father and appeals to them to believe in the evidence of their own eyes. He and the work he does cannot be separated from his Father.

FIFTH WEEK OF LENT – SATURDAY

Readings: Ezekiel 37:21-28; John 11:45-56

He prophesied … that Jesus would die for the nation, and not only for the nation but so that the scattered children of God might be gathered into one.

John 11:51-52

In his vision for the future of God's people, the prophet Ezekiel looks to the day when the nation will again be reunited under a descendant of King David. After the death of Solomon, sharp divisions emerged within Israel resulting in the division of the nation into the Northern and Southern kingdoms, each with its own ruler (1 Kings 12). The prophet now envisages the return of the scattered exiles to their own homeland and heritage, accompanied by a profound spiritual renewal, and one that would be marked by the abiding presence of almighty God in their midst. The ancient promise God made to David (2 Sam 7) again finds expression with the prophecy that a royal Davidic descendant would be the focus of unity for a single people. This splendid picture of Ezekiel forms part of the background to the passage from John which is the Gospel of the day.

For the Jewish religious and political leaders a crisis point had now been reached. The followers that Jesus was attracting through the authoritative nature of his preaching, as well as the divisions he caused among the people, impelled them to deliberate and take action. Fearing for the future of the nation at the hands of the Romans, they decided to put Jesus to death. In a scene replete with irony we hear the High Priest say that it is better for one man to die, rather than that the whole nation should perish. The Evangelist notes the prophetic character of Caiaphas' words, that Christ would die not only for his own people but, in fulfilment of Ezekiel's prophecy, to gather into one all God's scattered children. John is here referring to the universal character of Christ's death as the Lamb of God who would take away the sins of the whole world.

Meditations

HOLY WEEK

HOLY WEEK – MONDAY

Readings: Isaiah 42:1-7; John 12:1-11

Mary brought in a jar of precious ointment, pure nard, and anointed the feet of Jesus.

John 12:3

Our opening reading from Isaiah on this Monday of Holy Week speaks of the servant chosen and sustained by God, the object of his delight and pleasure. As the passage unfolds, the gentle and unobtrusive features of this servant become clear. Those most in need of a helping hand, summed up in the expression '*the bruised reed or the wavering flame*' have nothing to fear from him. His task will be to mediate something of God's truth and justice to a world waiting expectantly for it. The Creator of all that exists has given his servant a mission which is universal in scope. God has set him apart and appointed him to be a covenant between God and the people, vividly described as 'a light to the nations'. He will be a teacher of the nations, and his divinely inspired instruction will lead them from the darkness of ignorance into the clear light of God's truth. The Church sees delineated in this oracle of Isaiah the figure of Christ the Messiah, an oracle which is a telling example of how almighty God spoke through the prophets to prepare the world for the coming of Jesus Christ.

A supper at the house of Martha and Mary six days before the Jewish Passover was a significant occasion for the Evangelists, as Matthew, Mark and John all record it. John's account follows Jesus' dramatic raising of Lazarus from the dead. When Mary proceeded to anoint the feet of the Lord Jesus with precious ointment as a sign of deep affection for her guest, Judas showed his disapproval and at the same time revealed something of his real character when he remarked that the money for the ointment would have been better spent by being given to the poor. In response, Christ reveals the true meaning of Mary's anointing: it was in preparation for his burial. Jesus, always supremely in command of the situation, was fully aware of what lay ahead of him. He knew that his 'hour' was near and that his time on earth was coming to an end.

HOLY WEEK – TUESDAY

Readings: Isaiah 49:1-6; John 13:21-33,36-38

Now has the Son of Man been glorified, and in him God has been glorified.

John 13:31

The servant of the Lord and his mission to the nations again provide the theme of our reading from the prophet Isaiah. In language similar to that of the call of Jeremiah (Jer 1), the servant has been chosen and called by God from his mother's womb. In the short dialogue contained in the passage, the doubts and misgivings expressed by the prophet are dismissed by God as he reveals to him the wider purpose he has in mind for him. The mission of the servant will not be confined to restoring the scattered and exiled tribes of Israel only, but will embrace all nations. As we heard in yesterday's reading from Isaiah, God intends his servant to shed the light of his salvation on all the peoples of the earth. The figure of the servant of the Lord as found in Isaiah speaks to us in Holy Week of Jesus Christ and his mission, who by his death and Resurrection was destined to bring God's saving purpose supremely to fulfilment.

The pain of betrayal by one of his chosen disciples weighed heavily on Jesus. The intimate setting of the

Last Supper room, described for us in John's Gospel, allows us to sense something of the atmosphere pervading the final meal Jesus would share with the Twelve. That one of those present would act treacherously caused dismay, and John highlights the role of Peter and the Beloved disciple in pinpointing who the betrayer was. The distress of Jesus is almost tangible, and as Judas departs to set in motion Jesus' arrest the Evangelist remarks that 'it was night'. The hour of darkness had arrived. Christ then proceeds to explain that what would befall him would lead to both his glory and that of his Father. For the tragic sequence of events now about to engulf Jesus Christ would ultimately result in his decisive and definitive victory over the power of evil and death. His Resurrection would disclose his true identity as the Son of the Father. Jesus was returning to the Father through the way of the cross. The rash assertions of Peter at table only serve to highlight the lonely fate of the Master.

HOLY WEEK – WEDNESDAY

Readings: Isaiah 50:4-9; Matthew 26:14-25

I did not rebel, nor did I turn away.

Isaiah 50:5

Our liturgy today presents to us the third so-called servant-song, drawn from the prophet Isaiah. The servant declares that he enjoys an intimate relationship with the Lord, instructing others from the divine truth that has been revealed to him. The servant of the Lord faces adversity with steadfastness, and does not shirk from the physical force levelled at him by his enemies. Placing his trust fully in God, he has the assurance of divine protection and the conviction that his righteous cause will ultimately prevail. In words that St Paul would echo much later in his Letter to the Romans (8:31), the servant asks if God is on his side who can be against him? With good reason Isaiah has on occasion been called the 'fifth Evangelist', so prophetically do his oracles seem to speak directly to us of Christ. When reading this particular passage the believer cannot fail to see a prophetic portrayal of the Passion of the Son of God.

As Jesus approaches the final Passover of his life, Matthew relates how Judas approached the authorities with an offer to betray him. The sum of money agreed, thirty silver pieces, is also found in a text of the prophet Zechariah (11:12), and seems to be a further instance of the Evangelist seeing even the smallest details in Christ's life predicted in Scripture. At the supper table Jesus agonises aloud about his coming betrayal, and that by one of those present who shared the Passover meal with him. He acknowledges and accepts that his destiny is marked out for him in the Scriptures, and which therefore express God's will in his regard. However, humanly speaking, Judas must bear responsibility for his grievous deed. The great drama of our salvation enacted in the cross and death of Christ illustrates God's inscrutable and almighty power, which ultimately prevails in spite of the tragedy of sin and human wilfulness.

HOLY WEEK – THURSDAY
MASS OF THE LORD'S SUPPER

Readings: Exodus 12:1-8,11-14;
1 Corinthians 11:23-26; John 13:1-15

I have given you an example: just as I have done to you, so you also should do to one another.

John 13:15

A solemnity pervades the Liturgy of the Word for the evening Mass of the Lord's Supper, appropriate to the Sacred Triduum now beginning. In the reading from Exodus Moses prescribes strict and precise regulations for the celebration of the Passover meal. The blood of the Paschal lamb sprinkled on the doorposts and lintels of their houses would cause the Destroyer to 'pass over', and so ward off the destructive plague from the Israelites in Egypt. This meal would be a memorial meal, to be celebrated by all succeeding generations in memory of the deliverance from Egyptian bondage.

Jesus and his disciples gathered to celebrate this Passover meal, as the apostle Paul records, on the night before he died. However, invested with his full authority as Son of God, He who came to fulfil the Law and the Prophets transformed and gave an entirely new meaning to this ancient celebration. By his word the unleavened bread and cup of wine became his body and blood, an anticipation of the sacrifice he would make of himself for his disciples on the cross the following day. His command was that they should imitate what he did and celebrate this meal in his memory. Paul adds that every time we do so, we are proclaiming the death of the Lord. Christ is our Passover lamb whose blood purifies and protects us. The old order has passed, the new has come.

In the Gospel the Evangelist John presupposes the institution of the Eucharist, and recounts instead the astonishing act of Jesus who washed the feet of his disciples. By a symbolic, prophet-like gesture, Christ was dramatising the meaning of the Eucharist and its profound implications of service for those who would share in this sacred food. By washing his disciples' feet he was demonstrating in the most vivid manner possible the depths of God's love, a love which they in turn must take to the world through the power drawn from the celebration of his holy Eucharist.

GOOD FRIDAY –
CELEBRATION OF THE LORD'S PASSION

Readings: Isaiah 52:13–53:12; Hebrews 4:14-16; 5:7-9;
John 18:1–19:42

*And carrying his own cross, he went out of the city to
the place called the skull, or as it is called in Hebrew,
Golgotha.*

John 19:17

The Good Friday liturgy opens with the remarkable
fourth and final servant-song from Isaiah. In a passage
of rare beauty and theological insight, the servant of
the Lord is described as an innocent victim who suffered
for the sins of his people. He bore his fate humbly and
with submission, accepting in his own person the
sufferings that the nation merited because of its sinful
behaviour before God. This meditative song from Isaiah
on the merit of vicarious suffering marks a high-point
in the Old Testament reflection on innocent suffering,
and exercised a profound influence on the New
Testament understanding and presentation of the Passion
of Christ. At the Last Supper Jesus spoke of his blood
being poured out for many (Mt 26:28), aware that he
himself through his Passion and death became the
servant of God in a unique way.

The reading from the letter to the Hebrews takes the theme of suffering further and is reassuring in what it teaches. Through his incarnation Christ, now our great high priest ministering before God on our behalf, can sympathise with weak and frail humanity because of the temptations and trials to which he himself was subject during his own life on earth. His self-surrender to suffering and death out of obedience to his Father has merited for us all the gifts and blessings of God's salvation. We have only to approach our advocate before God with confidence.

The story of the Passion as told by John presents a dignified Christ who is at the mercy of others, while at the same time fully in command of his situation, even in the presence of Pilate, the Roman Governor. He takes up his cross willingly and of his own accord (19:17), going freely to his place of death. He arranges for his mother to be cared for, entrusting her into the hands of the beloved disciple (19:25-27), while exhorting the disciple to look on Mary as a mother. His life's work was now accomplished (19:30), and at a moment and time of his own choosing he bowed his head and yielded up his spirit.

THE EASTER VIGIL

Readings: Genesis 1:1-2:2; 22:1-18; Exodus 14:15-15:1;
Isaiah 54:5-14. 55:1-11; Baruch 3:9-15,32-4:4;
Ezekiel 36:16-28; Romans 6:3-11

Year A	–	Matthew 28:1-10;
Year B	–	Mark 16:1-7
Year C	–	Luke 24:1-12

He is not here. He has risen, just as he said he would.
Matthew 28:6

"Therefore let us watch and pray, so that we may celebrate this vigil both internally and externally. Let God speak to us through his Scriptures, and let us speak to God in our prayers. If we listen obediently to his words, the One to whom we pray will live in us."
St Augustine, Sermon 219,1

From earliest times the Easter Vigil has been called the Mother of all Vigils because of its central place in the liturgical life of the Church. Moses prescribed to the people of Israel that the feast of the Passover should mark the beginning of all months (Ex 12:1), and similarly the night of Christ's own Passover from death to Resurrection is the climax of the Church's year. No other celebration can compare with it. The ceremony of light with which the Vigil begins, followed by the singing of the Exultet beside the newly-lit Easter candle, proclaims the triumph of the light of life over the darkness of death. As St Augustine would have expressed it, 'with Christ's Resurrection the eternal day has broken into our temporal day.'

The Liturgy of the Word tonight recounts for us in magisterial fashion God's mighty deeds and promises throughout history on behalf of his people. This comprehensive historical sweep of God's saving deeds reaches definitive fulfilment in the greatest of all demonstrations of his sovereign power: the life, death and Resurrection of his Son, Jesus Christ.

The majestic account of the creation of the world takes us back to the beginning of all things, inspiring within the listener a profound sense of wonder and awe. Acting supremely alone, the Lord God draws order out of the primeval chaos and with assured deliberation gradually confers a pattern and meaning on the vast structure of the universe. The creation story is marked by harmony and a sense of purpose, with both animate and inanimate beings given their own proper place and function by God. Man and woman, different from the rest of the created order through being made in God's own image and likeness, represent the summit of the divine creative work. From the perspective of faith, we understand how that unique bond now established between the

Creator and humanity would, in the fullness of time, be given its fullest expression when Jesus Christ, the Son of God, himself became a man.

The mystery of God's love for the world is foreshadowed in the account of the sacrifice of Abraham in tonight's second reading. The patriarch is mysteriously summoned by God to offer his son Isaac in sacrifice, and he faithfully and unquestioningly prepares to obey God's command. The long-awaited son, Abraham's sole hope for the future, was now to be offered on the altar of sacrifice. The tense and dramatic setting of this strange episode is further heightened by the child's innocence and his father's unyielding, even blind, faith in God. Abraham surmounted this supreme test of faith and was rewarded with the renewal of the divine promises of land and posterity. The lamb which he offered was an anticipation and reminder of that Lamb of God who takes away the sins of the world. This compelling story of Abraham and Isaac is for us an evocative and compelling image of God the Father and his beloved Son; a God who, in the words of St Paul, 'did not spare his own Son, but gave him up for us all' (Rom 8:32).

A cardinal moment in the life of the chosen people was their miraculous crossing of the Red Sea, the Exodus. The Israelites throughout their long history would always cherish the memory of the Exodus, regarding it as their great national epic and God's stupendous intervention on behalf of his beleaguered people. God's deliverance of Israel at the Red Sea enabled them to pass from freedom and oppression to a new future of freedom and promise. The enduring Exodus image serves to describe Christ's passage by the power of the Father through the dark night of death to the new life of the Resurrection. As the renewal of our baptismal promises on this night forcefully reminds us, we too have undergone our own Exodus with Christ in his death and Resurrection. Through the waters of baptism we have passed from death to life with him and have become a new creation, possessing in the Spirit the first-fruits of the eternal life to come.

The ringing declaration of Isaiah the prophet that God is unwavering in fidelity to his people constitutes the theme of the fourth reading of the Easter Vigil. The imminent return of the exiles from Babylon with a future of promise and restoration, one described in highly poetic terms, will be seen as a solid pledge of God's faithfulness and unerring purpose. As Christians we hear these prophecies addressed to us in a wholly new way. Enlightened by faith, we now know that Israel alone would not be the sole recipient of these promises of salvation. God's pity and compassion were destined to transcend Israel and embrace all nations. In Jesus Christ, crucified and risen, all peoples would be invited to share in God's blessings.

The fifth reading portrays the Lord God, speaking through the prophet Isaiah, extending an open invitation to a feast of free food and drink, to a food God alone can provide and which is enduring and satisfying. Isaiah exhorts Israel to return to God where her true interests are to be found, for he alone is the source of her life. Israel will then rediscover her role in God's plan to mediate his covenantal blessings to the peoples of the earth. Just as the rain and snow are effective in ensuring nature's growth and harvest so, proclaims God, will his all-powerful word unerringly succeed in its appointed mission. The text from Isaiah speaks of God's unfathomable purpose which is impossible for human beings to discern. Nowhere is the deeply mysterious nature of God's ways more evident than in the reality of the Word made flesh, whose death and Resurrection form the heart of the Easter Vigil liturgical celebration. The apostle Paul would later exclaim in his Letter to the Romans, *'O the depths and riches of the wisdom and knowledge of God! How deep are his judgements and unsearchable his ways!'* (Rom 11:33).

The sixth reading of the Easter Vigil is taken from Baruch and belongs to the Wisdom tradition of Scripture. Baruch addresses a people in exile and teaches that the reason for their predicament is because they have abandoned God, the fountain of wisdom. The Creator of the universe has revealed himself to Israel, and her possession of the Law makes her a very privileged people. Attachment to God's law will bring life, while spiritual death awaits those who depart from his revealed will. Now in the paschal mystery of his Son, Jesus Christ, the God of the universe has revealed his power and his wisdom in a manner surpassing the vision of the prophets. The deep symbolism of the Easter Vigil, especially the themes of light and water, suggests the abundance of divine life now made freely accessible in Christ to the whole world.

The seventh and final reading from the Old Testament is drawn from Ezekiel. In lofty and exalted tones the prophet foretells the certain restoration and return of God's people from exile through an entirely new dispensation ordained by God himself, and a home-coming marked by a deep and enduring spiritual renewal. Ever faithful to himself and his own truthfulness, the Lord God will permit neither the sinfulness of his people nor the tragedies of history to thwart his plan of salvation for Israel. Ezekiel's oracles announcing spiritual transformation with the accompanying themes of clean water, a new heart and a new spirit, have a particular resonance for the Christian faithful assembled for the Easter Vigil. The Church teaches that we become a new creation in the waters of baptism, sanctified by the death and Resurrection of Christ the Saviour. Easter is a time to recall the deep roots of our own spiritual death and rebirth in Christ.

The close association of baptism and Easter is underlined by the celebrated passage from St Paul's Letter to the Romans. The believer enters into the paschal mystery of Jesus Christ through baptism and now has a share in the rich inheritance of God's people. So intimate is the bond between Christ and those baptised that the apostle articulates it in terms of a death, burial and resurrection along with Christ. Paul draws here on the rich treasury of Scriptural themes from the Old Testament, especially those of communion and life with God. The apostle concludes that the Christian community's manner of life and ethical behaviour must henceforth reflect the newness of life we now share with the risen Lord.

The Liturgy of the Word for the Easter Vigil concludes with the synoptic Gospels at one in their witness to the truth of the Lord's Resurrection. Even after two thousand years the confusion and excitement of the disciples on that first Easter morning still shine through. Common to all the Gospels is the dawning realisation that the story of Jesus of Nazareth did not end with his burial. The startling declaration of the angel, 'He is not here, he has risen', heralds the final and definitive chapter of the story of our salvation. That story will continue until Jesus Christ, the Son of God, returns again in glory.

'*For if God did not spare his own Son, but gave him up for us all, how will he not give us everything else with him?*' (Rom 8:32) Christ has suffered, let us die to sin; Christ has risen, let us live for God. Christ has passed from this world to the Father; let not our hearts cling to what belongs to this earth, but rather follow him to the things above. Our Head has hung on the cross, let us crucify the desires of the flesh; he lay in the tomb: buried together with him let us forget what is past; he is seated in heaven, let us raise our desires to higher things (St Augustine, Sermon 229D, 1).

Meditations

SUNDAYS OF LENT
AND PASSION SUNDAY
(Years A, B & C)

FIRST SUNDAY OF LENT – YEAR A

Readings: Genesis 2:7-9. 3:1-7; Romans 5:12-19;
Matthew 4:1-11

*For just as by the disobedience of one man many were
made sinners, so by the obedience of one man will many
be made righteous.*

Romans 5:19

The liturgy of this first Sunday of Lent sets the stage for
the unfolding of the great drama of our salvation in
Christ. We hear in Genesis how God the Creator placed
man and woman in Eden, endowed with every good
thing they could possibly want. Yet the power of
temptation proved too strong for Adam and Eve, and
they succumbed to the illusion that they could be like
gods, autonomous, if they were to partake of the fruit
God had forbidden them to eat. Their act of disobedience brought them nothing but the shameful
knowledge that they both were naked. Sin had now
entered the world with immense implications for the
children of Adam and Eve.

In the theologically developed extract from his Letter
to the Romans, St Paul had this Genesis passage very
much in mind. The apostle contrasts the harm inflicted
on mankind by the sin of Adam with the free gift of
grace brought by Christ. The transgression of the first

Adam, which brought sin and consequently death into the world, cannot be compared to the gracious deed of Jesus Christ which has become the source of life and abundant divine grace. As descendants of sinful Adam we stood condemned, but God has now repealed the sentence and made us righteous in Christ.

The Evangelist Matthew relates how Jesus, after his baptism and under the impulse of the Spirit, spent forty days in the wilderness wrestling with the temptations of the devil. Our first parents yielded to temptation; not so Jesus Christ. Satan laid out before him enticing attractions, such as the adulation of others and worldly power, but through his struggles and intense prayer Jesus came to understand that such enticements were not in keeping with his Father's will, the supreme rule of his life. He knew that a different road lay ahead of him and which would indeed lead to glory and exaltation, but by way of the cross. By rejecting the temptations of the prince of this world, Jesus' redemptive work as the second Adam had begun.

FIRST SUNDAY OF LENT – YEAR B

Readings: Genesis 9:8-15; I Peter 3:18-22;
Mark 1:12-15

The time is fulfilled, and the Kingdom of God is near.
Repent and believe the Gospel.

Mark 1:15

Baptism in water and the Holy Spirit marks the beginning of our Christian life. The call of Lent is for God's people to grow in their appreciation of the sacrament of baptism. Today's first reading describes God's covenant with Noah and all living creatures, when God swore never again to allow the earth to be destroyed by water. The apostle Peter in his first letter, an epistle widely understood as being addressed to those newly-baptised, sees the destructive waters of the great flood in Noah's day as prefiguring Christian baptism.

The transformation that baptism brings about in the soul of the believer derives from the power of Christ's death and Resurrection. The risen Lord is the source of that new life which we make our own through fidelity to our baptismal promises. Or as St Peter expresses it in our second reading, *A pledge made to God from a good conscience.* Noah and his family stood out through their faith in God. The Christian likewise, through being incorporated into Christ's death and

Resurrection, is delivered from the destruction of selfishness and sin. We will be asked to renew our baptismal promises at Easter. Having made the spiritual journey through Lent the Church prays that we may do so with a good conscience.

The Evangelist Mark records in the briefest detail the story of the Lord's temptation in the wilderness, but he is at one with Matthew and Luke in stating that the Spirit inspired Jesus to engage in this struggle with Satan. As we begin our Lenten penance and start our journey towards Easter, we have before us the example of the Son of God who felt the necessity for denial and self-sacrifice in order to prepare himself for the work entrusted to him by his Father. Mark adds, that after his period in the wilderness, Jesus began his public ministry with the call for a change of heart and faith in the message of the good news from God that he was proclaiming. That summons of Christ to a new way of living and full acceptance of his gospel has lost none of its urgency.

FIRST SUNDAY OF LENT – YEAR C

Readings: Deuteronomy 26:4-10; Romans 10:8-13;
Luke 4:1-13

You shall worship the Lord your God, and serve him alone.

Luke 4:8

The model for the spiritual journey we call Lent derives from that period of forty days Christ spent praying and fasting in the Judean wilderness. The gospels record how during that time he was severely tempted by the devil. Both Matthew and Luke give detailed accounts of the temptations, whereas Mark simply notes the fact that Jesus was tempted. The manner in which Jesus dealt with the tempter serves as an encouragement and inspiration to us who have to struggle with temptation and sin in all its many forms. The cunning of the devil is exposed through the manner in which he cites Scripture to bolster his attempts to lead Jesus astray. Paramount in the life of Jesus Christ was the will of his heavenly Father, and not even in this critical situation would he allow himself to deviate from that will. Likewise for us Christians, the challenge of Lent is to allow the sovereign will of God to become the supreme norm of our lives.

The reading from the book of Deuteronomy is in reality a profession of faith made by the pious Israelite, acknowledging the wonders God has done for his people since the beginning. St Paul teaches us in his Letter to the Romans that by professing our faith in the God who raised Jesus from the dead we stand justified in his eyes. All people of every race have now free access to God. We have only to believe to be saved.

The picture of the solitary Christ in the wilderness, confronted by temptation and the lure of all that could lead him astray from the realm of his Father, underlines the reality of the incarnation of the Son of God and his complete identification with the human condition. The Fathers of the Church were fond of enunciating the principle that 'What was not assumed, was not redeemed', referring to Christ's sharing in all that we human beings experience. As we wrestle with our own particular demons during these forty days, we keep our eyes firmly fixed on him who has been tempted in every way that we are, Jesus Christ (Heb 4:15).

SECOND SUNDAY OF LENT – YEAR A

Readings: Genesis 12:1-4; 2 Timothy 1:8-10;
Matthew 17:1-9

Lord, it is wonderful for us to be here.

Matthew 17:4

The conviction and belief of the first Christians was that in Jesus Christ the Scriptures of Israel reached their complete fulfilment. We hear in our Gospel on this second Sunday of Lent how, on the mount of Transfiguration, Moses and Elijah appeared alongside Jesus, speaking with him. The writings we have come to know as the Law and the Prophets were believed to contain the perfect expression of God's will for his people. In a scene reminiscent of the giving of the Law on Mount Sinai (Ex 19), the Father affirms that Jesus is his own beloved Son and to him we must now listen. His teaching as the Son of the Father both perfects and surpasses that of the Law and the Prophets, represented on the mountain by the towering biblical figures of Moses and Elijah. The vision of Jesus in glory, which so overwhelmed the three disciples, highlighted the uniqueness of his person, and intimated that a new and definitive era in God's saving dealings with humanity had arrived. As Son, Christ could speak with an authority that neither Moses nor any of the prophets could lay claim to.

Writing to Timothy, Paul speaks of the grace God had decreed to grant us before time began and which has now been revealed with the appearance of Jesus Christ. The season of Lent for us is meant to be a journey of rediscovery, of wonder at God's graciousness towards us, something that was planned from eternity. We can never ponder sufficiently the significance of the life, death and Resurrection of Jesus Christ, through which a loving God speaks to us most eloquently. Faithful Abraham was called by God to embark on a new path and set out into the unknown. He was bidden to leave behind all that he knew and cherished, and so discover a new future he could hardly have dreamed of. Abraham had the courage to accept the challenge and to place his trust in God. He remains a model for all believers.

SECOND SUNDAY OF LENT – YEAR B

Readings: Genesis 22:1-2,9-13,15-18;
Romans 8:31-34; Mark 9:2-10

This is my beloved Son. Listen to him.

Mark 9:7

The figure of an only son is central to all three Scriptural readings on this second Sunday of Lent. In the passage from Genesis, the patriarch Abraham is mysteriously commanded by God to sacrifice his son Isaac. Abraham had waited long for the son promised by God, and now he was being asked to sacrifice him, and with him all his hopes for the future. The greatness of Abraham lay in his unshakeable obedience and firm faith in God. As we hear, his faith was not misplaced. Isaac was spared and Abraham's posterity assured.

The sacrifice of Isaac foreshadows that of Christ, God's own Son. With this in mind, the apostle Paul asks how could we doubt God's infinite love for us when he did not even spare his own Son, but handed him over to death for all of us? Abraham was spared the pain of sacrificing his son; God the Father's love for the human race took him further when he allowed his Son to become the sacrificial lamb on the cross. Our confidence in God therefore, the apostle declares, should be unbounded.

The transfiguration scene, as found in Mark, reveals Jesus Christ as the one who came to put the seal on the Law and the Prophets by conferring on them their true and definitive meaning. The presence of Moses and Elijah with Jesus on the mountain demonstrates his continuity with these outstanding servants of God, while the words of the Father affirming that Jesus is truly his Son and the one to whom we must now listen, demonstrate that his teaching now surpasses that of Moses and Elijah. Israel awaited the fulfilment of God's ancient promise that he would one day raise up another prophet like Moses who would speak God's words to them (Deut 18:18). In the presence and ministry of Jesus Christ that promise has been realised in a surpassing way, because he is the Son of God. The splendour of Christ's Transfiguration serves to confirm our faith in the truth that it was the Word of God himself who became flesh and took up his dwelling among us.

SECOND SUNDAY OF LENT – YEAR C

Readings: Genesis 15: 5-12, 17-18;
Philippians 3:17-4:1; Luke 9-28-36

This is my Son, the chosen one. Listen to him!

Luke 9:35

The unity which is Sacred Scripture, a 'seamless garment', becomes evident from the story of the Transfiguration which provides the Gospel reading on this second Sunday of Lent. The account is rich in biblical allusions. The scene unfolds on a mountain, a traditional and historical place of encounter with God. While he was at prayer, Moses and Elijah appear alongside Jesus. Luke records that they conversed with him about his forthcoming 'exodus' in Jerusalem, a clear reference to his Passion and death and which would constitute his own personal Passover from this world to his Father. On Mount Sinai Moses gave God's law to Israel, and later the prophet Elijah would prove to be a stalwart defender of the religion of Israel in the face of pagan worship. Their presence with Jesus on the mount of Transfiguration shows how Jesus came to bring to fulfilment the work of Moses and the prophets as recounted in the Scriptures. This he would accomplish through his suffering, death and Resurrection. The cloud covering the mountain, together with the sound of the Father's voice affirming Christ's divine sonship, recall the appearance of God to Moses on Sinai, (Ex 19), and that to Elijah on Mount Horeb when he encountered God in a 'gentle breeze' (1 Kings 19:1-14). Jesus Christ is the golden thread running through the whole of Sacred Scripture, *the yes to all of God's promises* (2 Cor 1:20).

The liturgical season of Lent, especially through the chosen Scriptural texts, leads us to a deeper under-standing of God's saving plan for the world. The ancient covenant with Abraham, as described in our first reading, provides proof of God's desire to reveal himself and his gracious designs. Abraham responded with whole-hearted faith to the divine initiative and found favour before God (Gen 15:6). His response remains the model for every believer. From Abraham onwards, Almighty God gradually unfolded his salvific will until it reached its climax in Jesus Christ. He would inaugurate in his blood the new and universal covenant between God and man. What began with the call of Abraham will reach final completion when, in Paul's words, Christ will return in glory to renew all things, even our mortal bodies (Phil 3:20).

THIRD SUNDAY OF LENT – YEAR A

Readings: Exodus 17:3-7; Romans 5:1-2,5-8;
John 4:5-42

If you but knew the gift of God…

John 4:10

The centrepiece of our Scripture readings on this Sunday of Lent is the encounter of Jesus with the Samaritan woman at the well as told in John's Gospel. The story is one of conversion, revolving around the theme of fresh, living water, and opens with Jesus' request to the woman for a drink of water. As the narrative unfolds, Jesus offers the woman living water for which she really thirsts but does not know it. In the carefully constructed dialogue Jesus gradually leads the Samaritan woman to a deeper perception of who is speaking to her. Her mention of the Samaritan belief that the Messiah would come and explain everything gave Jesus the opening to declare that he himself was the Messiah who was speaking to her (Jn 4:25-26).

The call to conversion and return to God lies at the heart of Lent, and this Gospel story is a fine example of a sinner gradually finding her way back to the Lord with her former style of life transformed. She has now become an evangelist among her own people! As a symbol that she had found the pearl of great price, the woman abandoned her water jar (v 28) and ran to tell others about the One she had discovered. The delicacy and sensitive manner in which Jesus treated the woman are intended to illustrate the mercy and pity that Christ has for all who have fallen from grace. As in the case of the Samaritan woman, he will slowly reveal himself to them and quench their thirst with the living water of his Spirit.

The cry of the wandering Israelites in Exodus for water to quench their thirst prepares us for the Gospel encounter of Jesus with the woman at the well. God granted his people's request and gave them water to satisfy their material needs for the moment. But it would be the Son of God himself who would provide the water that would endure and which would finally lead to eternal life. St Paul captures neatly what Jesus meant by the pledge of living water springing up to eternal life, when he refers in our second reading to the love of God being poured into our hearts through the Holy Spirit who has been given to us. In Christ we already have the first-fruits of the Spirit, the living water, and now await its fullness in the life to come.

THIRD SUNDAY OF LENT – YEAR B

Readings: Exodus 20:1-17; 1 Corinthians 1:22-25;
John 2:13-25

Jesus said, 'Destroy this temple and in three days I will raise it up'.

John 2:19

The cleansing of the Jerusalem Temple as recorded by the Evangelist John represented a deeply symbolic act on the part of Jesus. At one level, and standing firmly within the tradition of the great prophets of Israel, Jesus was condemning the abuses associated with this most sacred place of worship. He was outraged at the manner in which traders and money-changers were defiling his Father's house. However, his own startling words on the destruction and restoration of the Temple reveal the true meaning of the incident, '*Destroy this temple and in three days I will raise it up.*' By speaking in this way, Jesus is making the claim that he himself is now the Temple of God, the locus of the divine presence on earth. In Jesus Christ, God the Father has inaugurated a new and definitive order of salvation. Referring to his coming death as the destruction of this Temple which he embodies in person, Jesus will demonstrate his divine power by raising it up after three days in the glory of his Resurrection. The full significance of Christ's words, the Evangelist notes, only became clear to the disciples after Christ had risen from the dead (v 22). Like the disciples, we too are called during our Lenten journey to grow in our understanding of the significance of Christ's death and Resurrection.

In the second reading the apostle Paul describes the cross as being a stumbling-block to the people of Israel, while the wisdom-seeking Greeks dismissed it as folly. The death of Christ on the cross mysteriously reveals the divine power at work, something which overturns all human values and pretensions. The self-emptying of Christ manifested in the crucifixion is the astonishing manifestation of God's love for the world, a truth the writers of the New Testament never cease to proclaim.

While Jesus came to replace the Temple in Jerusalem by his own life and ministry, he also endorsed and elevated to a higher level what was finest and best in the teaching of the Law and the Prophets of God's people. The Decalogue proclaimed for us today in the book of Exodus remains definitive as a moral standard for our Christian living. In Jesus' own words, *'I have come not to abolish the Law but to fulfil it'* (Mt 5:17).

THIRD SUNDAY OF LENT – YEAR C

Readings: Exodus 3:1-8,13-15;
1 Corinthians 10:1-6,10-12; Luke 13:1-9

I say to you, unless you repent you will all likewise perish.

Luke 13:3

The fundamental Lenten theme of repentance figures prominently in the liturgical readings of this Sunday. In the biblical understanding of the term, to repent means to undergo a change of heart and embrace a totally new way of living. The Gospel passage from Luke records Christ summoning the crowds to repentance and to accept responsibility for their lives, otherwise it will be too late and their fate will be no better than the Galileans mentioned in the story. The very presence of Christ on earth is a summons to look at things differently, to lay aside our own prejudices and presuppositions, and to accept the offer of God's salvation which he has come to proclaim. The message of the little parable of the barren fig tree is to repent while we have the opportunity, for we may not always have it. Lent is a wake-up call!

The apostle Paul urges the believers in Corinth to learn from the lessons of the past. The events surrounding the crossing of the sea at the Exodus under

Moses represented a baptism of a kind for the people of Israel. God also provided them with spiritual food and water from the rock, nevertheless, despite these blessings their hearts were wayward and they perished in the desert. Paul goes on to say that all of this was written down as a warning to us. We have the privileges of baptism and the food of the holy Eucharist, but we must ensure that we derive the full benefits of these foundational sacraments. The fate of the generation in the wilderness stands as a salutary warning to all subsequent generations.

Our response to the call of Christ expressed through repentance forms but part of a wider picture. The appearance of God to Moses in the burning bush shows how God has first taken the initiative in the great drama of our salvation. He has, as it were, taken the first step and come in search of us. Initially he came to Moses and the people of Israel to deliver them from bondage and open up a new life of freedom to them in a land of their own. This gracious and loving design of almighty God was, however, ultimately destined to extend to all the peoples of the earth.

The First Letter of John captures this truth well, *Let us love, because God has loved us first,* (1 Jn 4:19). These inspired words take us to the very heart of our Lenten endeavours.

FOURTH SUNDAY OF LENT – YEAR A

Readings: 1 Samuel 16:1,6-7,10-13; Ephesians 5:8-14;
John 9:1-41

*Jesus said to him, "Go and wash in the pool of Siloam,
a name which means 'sent'."*

John 9:7

The extended narrative in John's Gospel of the healing
of the man who was blind from birth has long been
understood as an image of Christian baptism and the
awakening of faith in the Son of God. The blind man
encounters Jesus and is told to go and bathe his eyes
in the pool called Siloam. The Evangelist adds the
significant detail that Siloam means 'sent'. There he
receives the gift of physical sight through the power of
the One sent by God, Jesus Christ. The various phases
of this story point to the man's growth in faith, despite
the difficulties placed in his path by the Pharisees who
would belittle the claims of Jesus. Through meeting
Christ and having his sight restored, the man caught a
glimpse of the spiritual truth that Jesus offered and
clung tenaciously to it. He did not shirk from witnessing
before the Pharisees to the reality of what had happened
to him, and was even prepared to accept the consequences of expulsion from the Jewish community.
The story reaches a climax with the man, at one time
both physically and spiritually blind, now discovering

the full identity of Jesus and confessing him as Lord. He had come to Jesus, obeyed his command to bathe in water, and now possessed the gift of sight in the deepest sense of the word.

The extract from Paul's Letter to the Ephesians could well serve as a commentary on the Gospel of this Sunday. The opposites of darkness and light depict life before baptism and the new life that Christ confers in the sacrament of baptism. To live a life independently of God is to remain in darkness, whereas to walk in the light of Christ is to leave the realm of death and share in the life of God. The choice of the young David as the Lord's anointed, recounted in the first book of Samuel, indicates how God was gradually preparing his people for the coming of his chosen Messiah in the fullness of time, his Son Jesus Christ. He would be anointed with the fullness of the Holy Spirit, and by his life, death and Resurrection, would bring the world from the darkness of sin and error into the realm of God's redemptive light. Lent is a grace-filled time for us to rediscover our baptismal roots.

FOURTH SUNDAY OF LENT – YEAR B

Readings: 2 Chronicles 36:14-16, 19-23;
Ephesians 2:4-10; John 3:14-21

*God so loved the world that he gave his only-begotten
Son.*

John 3:16

The inspired words of John in this Sunday's Gospel
passage take us to the very heart of the Christian faith,
which is the immensity of God's love for the world
which impelled him to give up his only Son lest we
perish in our sins. The dramatic story of God's dealings
with humanity as recorded in Scripture finds its ultimate
explanation in the mystery and wonder of the divine
love. Yet that love was demonstrated in the most
unexpected way, in the cross of Jesus Christ. The
Evangelist understood the incident of the bronze serpent
during Israel's desert wanderings, (Num 21:6-9) as
prefiguring Christ on the cross. Just as the act of fixing
their gaze on the bronze serpent brought healing to the
stricken Israelites, so the believer looking on the
crucified One with the eye of faith will find God's
salvation.

The liturgy of Ash Wednesday highlighted the need to
repent and to turn away from our sins. We miss the
point if we view this Lenten call as a one-sided affair,

somehow contingent on our own often feeble efforts. Both John and the apostle Paul insist most emphatically that the love of God which is given to us in Christ precedes all our own accomplishments. The utterly gratuitous and unmerited nature of what God has done for us through his Son is described by Paul as 'grace'. The discipline and exercises of Lent are meant to attune us to the astonishing nature of God's bountiful love etched graphically for us in the life, death and Resurrection of his Son, Jesus Christ.

The extract from the book of Chronicles should serve as an encouragement to us that with God a future and a new beginning will always be possible. Jerusalem, the holy city, lay in ruins but the emergence through divine providence of a new king, Cyrus, heralded a fresh beginning and an era of restoration for God's people. Our own struggles with sin and temptation must therefore never cause us to be despondent and disheartened. The saving purpose of God will always prevail, as was so powerfully proved in the cross of Christ, and eloquently expressed in the words of the ancient hymn, 'God reigned from a tree'.

FOURTH SUNDAY OF LENT – YEAR C

Readings: Joshua 5:9-12; 2 Corinthians 5:17-23;
            Luke 15:1-3,11-32

Anyone who is in Christ is a new creation; the old order has passed away; behold the new one has come!
2 Corinthians 5:17

Common to all three Scripture readings on this Fifth Sunday of Lent is the idea of the old order giving way to an entirely new dispensation. On arriving in the land of promise, Canaan, the people of Israel no longer needed manna. God would now provide for them in another way, from the produce of their new homeland. The apostle Paul, writing to the Corinthians, goes so far as to speak of a new creation which has come about through the reconciling work of Jesus Christ. Employing the most daring language, the Apostle declares that in order to effect this reconciliation *God has made the sinless one into sin* (2 Cor 5:21). Such reconciliation is unmerited and comes as God's free gift to us. Christ, by his cross, has taken upon himself our guilt and our sin so that we can stand justified before God. Much of this fine Pauline passage was read to us in our Ash Wednesday liturgy, calling us to embrace God's offer of reconciliation. We hear that call afresh today and are invited to respond.

Among the best known of all Jesus' parables, the story of the prodigal or wasteful son may be seen as an explanation in visual images of St Paul's teaching. The younger son leaves the security of his Father's house, determined on a life of so-called freedom and reckless living. Only when his resources were exhausted did he decide, much chastened, to return to his Father, resolved to do even the most menial tasks. The extent and warmth of the welcome he received from his Father almost defies human understanding. The Father's unbounded joy in having his son back home far outweighed any other consideration. Our return home to God, our loving Father, has been made possible by the self-emptying love of Jesus Christ, demonstrated by his death on the cross. Looking at his Son, God no longer holds our sins and faults against us. So far-reaching has been this redeeming work of Christ that it has resulted in a new creation. In Christ we stand newly created before God.

FIFTH SUNDAY OF LENT – YEAR A

Readings: Ezekiel 37:12-14; Romans 8:8-11;
John 11:1-45

Jesus said to Martha, 'I am the resurrection and the life.'

John 11:25

The Evangelist John brings the first part of his Gospel to a climax with the raising of Lazarus from the dead. The signs wrought by Jesus, the term favoured by John to describe the miracles of Jesus, were elemental symbols of the divine life which he came to give to the world. The marriage feast at Cana was the scene of an abundance of new wine, a prophetic promise for the last times. By healing the paralytic Jesus indicated that the Kingdom of God with its healing and wholeness had now arrived, while the feeding of the five thousand presaged the institution of the holy Eucharist, a spiritual food which would represent a genuine foretaste of the coming messianic banquet. Jesus came to bring God's light to a darkened world, and this finds powerful expression in the restoration of both physical and spiritual sight to the man blind from birth. These signs coalesce in the most fundamental sign of all: the bestowal of life as powerfully illustrated in the raising of Lazarus. John, referring to the Word Incarnate, had already stated in the Prologue that, *'In him was life'* (1:4). The

Lazarus story offers a dramatic and visual illustration of that statement.

In today's first reading, the exilic prophet Ezekiel presents the return of God's people from Babylon to their own land in the imaginative language of resurrection and new life. The Lord God would revive his people's fortunes after the desolation and pain of exile. A new and brighter future now opened up before the scattered Israelites. An enduring tenet of Israel's faith was that life, both physical and spiritual, was the preserve of God alone. From the standpoint of the unity of Sacred Scripture, such a passage from Ezekiel helped prepare the way for the full revelation of the resurrection and eternal life found in Jesus Christ, crucified and risen from the dead.

The apostle Paul explained to the Romans that there is a real sense in which even in the present time we can be alive or dead. To live in sin means being alienated from God and is a form of death, whereas to strive after spiritual things under the influence of God's Spirit brings life, and carries with it the sure promise of eternal life.

FIFTH SUNDAY OF LENT – YEAR B

Readings: Jeremiah 31:31-34; Hebrews 5:7-9;
John 12:20-33

*Truly, truly I say to you, unless a grain of wheat falls
into the ground and dies it remains a single grain; but if
it dies it bears much fruit.*

John 12:24

The request of some Jewish-Greek pilgrims in Jerusalem
to see Jesus was the signal for him that his 'hour' had
now arrived. At the wedding in Cana he had told his
mother that his hour had not yet come (Jn 2:4), and in
subsequent discourses he would frequently allude to
his hour. For John the Evangelist, what Jesus meant by
his hour was the hour of his Passion, which necessarily
led to his glorification. Passion and glory are but two
aspects of a single event and in the thought of the
Fourth Gospel are inseparable. The Greeks, who are
representative here of the wider pagan world, could
only see Jesus when he had been 'lifted up'. In other
words, only when Jesus had triumphed over death and
shown himself to be the glorified Lord in his Resurrection
would he be accessible in faith to the men and women
of every place and time on earth.

The striking image of the necessity of the wheat grain
lying dead deep in the earth prior to the harvest indicates

· 132 ·

just how conscious Jesus was of his coming death. He was also only too aware of the manner of that death: crucifixion, a fact to which the Evangelist today specifically draws our attention (12:33). The reading from the letter to the Hebrews casts further light into the mind of Jesus as he entered into his Passion. In a way in which we today find hard to comprehend, the Lord Jesus embraced suffering and death as a Son, out of loving obedience to his Father. Yet in God's saving design, his obedience was crowned by his becoming the saviour of the world. As we move into the season of Passiontide the liturgy increasingly focuses our attention on the figure of the suffering Christ, who renounced his own life so that we might have life in abundance.

The prophetic vision of a new covenant given by God, a covenant in which the divine law would be inscribed on human hearts rather than on tablets of stone, was one with which Jesus was familiar. At the Last Supper table he spoke of his coming death, in sacrificial terms through the offering of his body and blood, as the inauguration of that new covenant promised long ago by Jeremiah the prophet. The fullness of time had now arrived, the hour of God's new and everlasting covenant with all peoples, sealed in the blood of his own beloved Son.

FIFTH SUNDAY OF LENT – YEAR C

Readings: Isaiah 43:16-21; Philippians 3:8-14;
John 8:1-11

*Neither do I condemn you. Go now, and do not sin
again.*

John 8:12

The words of the apostle Paul to the Philippians in the
second reading, about forgetting the past and striving
for what lies ahead, summarise neatly the message of
this Sunday's Liturgy of the Word. Harking back to
Israel's great moment of deliverance at the Red Sea,
the prophet Isaiah announces that God is about to
perform another mighty deed on behalf of his people.
God would show his mighty power once more, only
this time by deliverance from exile and a safe return to
their homeland, through a wasteland whose harsh
conditions God will specifically soften for his returning
exiles. The imagery of Exodus and return capture well
the Lenten drama of the Christian soul as one of return
from the wilderness of sin and selfishness to a new
beginning under Christ.

As a devout member of the chosen people, Paul of
Tarsus had much to be proud of and his Jewish
credentials were impeccable. Yet once he encountered
Christ, or as he would have expressed it, when Christ

encountered him, all that he once cherished and held dear paled into insignificance. His one goal now was to know Christ and to grow ever more aware of the power of his Lord's risen, divine life. For Paul the past had become a foreign country. The person of Jesus Christ, the Son of God, had transformed everything, and for the apostle marked a beginning that was as profound as it was new.

The gracious and forgiving encounter of Christ with the adulterous woman in the Gospel also meant that, as with the exiled Israelites and Paul the Jew, she no longer felt burdened with her past. She found mercy and fresh hope where she might have expected reproach and condemnation. Christ welcomed her back home and offered her the possibility of a new life. The Lenten message to us rings clear from the readings today. We are to let go of our sinful past and accept God's offer in Christ to begin afresh. Christ will not condemn us. We are to go and sin no more.

PASSION SUNDAY

Readings: Isaiah 50:4-7; Philippians 2:6-11

Gospel   Year A   Matthew 26:14–27:66
         Year B   Mark 14:1–15:47
         Year C   Luke 22:14–23:56

Although he was in the form of God … he emptied himself, assuming the condition of a slave.

Philippians 2:6

The climax of this Sunday's Liturgy of the Word comes with the proclamation of the Passion of the Lord. Despite some differences of emphasis, the Passion accounts in all four Gospels are remarkably similar. The readings preceding the Gospel help set the scene. We hear the disciple of the Lord musing aloud in Isaiah. Listening carefully to what the Lord God says to him in prayer, the servant's mission consists in encouraging the weary and dispirited. The task laid on him by God will involve hostility and even violence, but remaining rock-like in his faith he will not be diverted from his prophetic calling. We inevitably see the figure and fate of Christ prefigured in this text from Isaiah.

Quoting from a very early Christian hymn in his Letter to the Philippians, the apostle Paul traces in a few lines the whole mystery of Christ. He was with God, but laying aside his divinity he became man, and plumbed the depths of humiliation through his death on the cross. But when the Father raised him from the dead all creation now acknowledges him as Lord, and this acknowledgement redounds to the glory of God the Father. This wonderfully dense Pauline passage adds an immeasurably rich dimension to our understanding of the Passion story.

PASSION SUNDAY – GOSPEL YEAR A

Writing his account with Jewish Christians in mind, the Evangelist Matthew highlights how the Scriptures were being fulfilled even through the tragic events of Christ's Passion. Matthew shared the conviction of the early Church that all of Scripture pointed to Christ. He was the Messiah whom God had long promised would come, and all that befell him was already to be found in the Scriptures we know as the Old Testament. When the disciples abandon Jesus, Matthew saw this long predicted in the prophet Zechariah (26:30-31), while he noted that the sum of thirty pieces of silver which Judas was paid for betraying Jesus had already been alluded to in the prophets (27:9-10). The saving plan of God for his people was to be discerned in the Scriptures, and consequently the sufferings and death of Christ were not fortuitous or simply the result of human wickedness. The brutal treatment and violent death that Jesus suffered were a mysterious part of a wider design of the Father for the salvation of the world, a plan which would only be fully disclosed in Christ's glorious and triumphant Resurrection from the dead.

PASSION SUNDAY – GOSPEL YEAR B

St Mark's narrative of the Passion is factual and straightforward. In common with the other Evangelists he makes no attempt to cover up the summary justice or to mitigate the brutal treatment Christ received before the Sanhedrin and at the hands of the Roman soldiers. Mark simply allows the story to speak for itself, and lets the reader draw the appropriate conclusions. In his description of the scene in the Garden of Gethsemane Jesus addresses his Father as 'Abba', an Aramaic term expressing the most intimate relationship between a son and his father. Here Mark gives us an insight into the prayer of Jesus as he faced the most critical hour of his life. Jesus' word of address to his Father, 'Abba', evokes all the trust and tenderness of a very special and unique relationship to God which he alone enjoyed. The apostle Paul would later teach that, because of the dignity conferred on us through our Christian baptism, we now enjoy the astounding privilege of addressing God the Father in the same way as his Son did, 'Abba, Father' (Rom 8:15; Gal 4:6).

PASSION SUNDAY – GOSPEL YEAR C

When listening to the four Gospel narratives of Christ's Passion we are struck by their factual and restrained nature. There is nothing overtly dramatic or exaggerated about them, and they are related in a sober and restrained manner. In Luke's account, mention should be made of how the Lord would pray for Peter against the wiles of the devil, so that Peter in turn might be a source of strength to his fellow disciples (Lk 22:31-32). Luke also records for us the consoling story of the repentant thief and Jesus' promise to him of a place in Paradise that very day (23:39-43). Listening to the Lord's last hours with faith, we journey with him and in a real sense make our own his sufferings and death for us and for the salvation of the whole world.

By the same author:

A Shoot from the Stock of Jesse

Meditations for Advent

During the season of Advent the Church sets before us a choice of Scriptural texts and antiphons to prepare us for the birthday of Christ our Saviour and Messiah. The period preceding Christmas is a busy one for many people nowadays and the spiritual dimension of Advent can easily be overlooked. In this little book Fr Michael Campbell offers us a daily Advent reflection based on one of the Scripture readings of the liturgy of the day. A few minutes of quiet reflection on the Word of God each day of Advent will lead us into a deeper understanding of the mystery of the Word made flesh, and so make the feast of Christmas spiritually so much more meaningful.

ISBN 0 85439 724 8   £4.50

ST PAULS